Jehovah's Witnesses

Answered
Verse by Verse

Jehovah's Witnesses
Answered
Verse by Verse

David A. Reed

BAKER BOOK HOUSE
Grand Rapids, Michigan 49506

Copyright 1986 by David A. Reed

ISBN: 0-8010-7739-7

Fourth printing, November 1987

Printed in the United States of America

Scripture references

ASV *American Standard Version.* © 1929 by International Council of
     Religious Education.
JB   *The Jerusalem Bible.* © 1966 by Darton, Longman & Todd, Ltd., and
     Doubleday & Company, Inc.
KJV *King James Version.*
LB   *The Living Bible.* © 1971 by Tyndale House Publishers, Wheaton,
     Illinois 60187.
MLB *Modern Language Bible* (Berkeley). © 1945, 1959, 1969 by the
     Zondervan Publishing House.
NIV *The Holy Bible, New International Version.* © 1978 by New York
     International Bible Society, used by permission of Zondervan Bible
     Publishers.
NWT *New World Translation of the Holy Scriptures.* © 1961, 1981, by
     Watch Tower Bible and Tract Society of Pennsylvania.
NKJV *New King James Version, Holy Bible.* © 1983 by Thomas Nelson, Inc.
RSV *Revised Standard Version.* © 1946, 1952, by Division of Christian
     Education of the Churches of Christ in the United States of
     America.

Contents

Introduction

They always manage to knock at the worst possible times—when you're still in bed on a Saturday morning, when the family has just sat down to Sunday dinner, when you're in the midst of bathing the baby—and they keep coming back with a persistence matched only by a hungry horsefly on a hot summer day. If you take the time to talk with them, they leave you frustrated and bewildered. They flip through their Bibles with amazing speed, quoting chapter and verse to "prove" that Jesus Christ is just an angel, that he died on an upright stake instead of on the cross, that accepting a blood transfusion is as sinful as adultery, and that the Watchtower Society in Brooklyn, New York, is God's modern-day "prophet," his "channel of communication."

How easy it is to think of Jehovah's Witnesses as evil incarnate and to drive them from the doorstep with a harsh rebuke! Occasionally, that is just what happens. My wife, Penni, who was raised a JW, once called with a younger trainee at the door of a man who identified himself as a Christian. As soon as he discovered who they were, he ordered them off his property, shouting "Deceivers!" and "Liars!" at the top of his voice and loudly condemning them to hell. (Penni used the episode to instruct her protégé on what church members are *really* like.)

More often, though, it is apathy rather than anger that greets the Witnesses at the doors. "I'm sorry. I'm not interested" is the response they hear most frequently, the next most common being "I'm sorry. I'm busy," or, somewhat less often, "I'm sorry. I'm a Methodist [or other denominational designation]." The JW will occasionally reply to the latter by saying, "I'm sorry, too, that you're a Methodist," but usually he or she will simply say, "Have a nice day!" and go on to the next house.

Why do they keep calling? For one thing, they believe that *you* will be destroyed in the imminent Battle of Armageddon unless you "come to Jehovah's organization for salvation" (*The Watchtower,* 11/15/81, p. 21). They are trying to save your life. But, even more so, the motivation that truly propels them is the belief that *they* will not survive Armageddon unless they engage in this door-to-door preaching work under the direction of "God's organization."

Most Jehovah's Witnesses are, in all sincerity, doing their best to serve God. They are like the unbelieving Jews of whom Paul wrote: ". . . they have a zeal of God, but not according to knowledge. For they being ignorant of God's righteousness, and going about to establish their own righteousness, have not submitted themselves unto the righteousness of God" (Rom. 10:2–3, KJV).

The vast majority of Jehovah's Witnesses are victims of victims—blind followers of blind leaders. They need to escape from the salvation-through-works treadmill that makes them obedient servants of a multibillion-dollar religious empire. They need liberation from the oppressive yoke that weighs down on their shoulders; yet they have been led to believe that it is the very carrying of that yoke that will save them—and that anyone who seeks to dissuade them is a deceiver sent by Satan.

If you have already made an attempt, then you realize how difficult it is to talk to Jehovah's Witnesses. They will try your patience, test your Bible knowledge, and strain

8

your endurance. Keeping track of the point under discussion with them can be as difficult as following the pea in a carnival huckster's shellgame, as they jump from one verse of Scripture to another. But the effort is worth it, because *they* need to hear the gospel from *you*.

Most JW's come from a life history devoid of spirituality. Large numbers had been Roman Catholics who seldom went to church. Some were raised in Protestant churches but never got the message. Many had no religious background at all and were living a life of materialism or sin— or simply felt trapped in a humdrum routine that led nowhere—and then the Witnesses knocked at the door. The invitation to "study the Bible" seemed attractive. God was what they needed in their life. But the Witnesses soon switched the "Bible study" to a Watchtower book study and led their new disciples to an idolized organization, instead of to God.

Who will help Jehovah's Witnesses hear the real gospel of Christ? Each week they knock at many doors and meet many people, including many Christians. But they seldom encounter anyone who wields "the sword of the Spirit" (Eph. 6:17) in such a way as to penetrate their mental fortress—that almost impenetrable wall of twisted reasoning that the Watchtower Society has erected in their brains. We Christians send missionaries to the most distant parts of the earth and train them to speak the most difficult languages, in order to reach the lost for Christ. Should we not also make at least some effort to speak effectively to these lost souls who come knocking at our very doors?

But a Christian who attempts to converse with Jehovah's Witnesses will need help. The JW's spend several hours each week studying and practicing for such encounters. So even a Bible reader who has a thorough knowledge of Scripture may be caught off guard by some of their strange arguments. If this happens, where will you

9

turn for help? It is to this end that the present volume has been prepared.

In it I have set out to examine closely the Jehovah's Witnesses' favorite Bible verses—the texts that they use as pretexts for teaching Watchtower doctrines. Each verse is considered from several angles. What do the JW's understand the verse to mean? How does it fit into their doctrinal framework? Is the verse mistranslated in their slanted Bible translation? Do they take it out of context? What does it really say? How can you best reason with a Witness on that passage?

Other verses selected for discussion include the ones Jehovah's Witnesses ignore—the texts that their leaders carefully avoid when conducting followers on a guided tour of the Bible. (Although I was a JW elder for eight years, responsible for teaching my own congregation and frequently serving as guest speaker at others, there were numerous passages in the Bible that I never knew existed—until the blinders were removed from my eyes.) This volume discusses the most significant of those verses and shows how you can use them effectively in sharing the gospel of Christ with a Witness.

For quick reference, the texts appear in the order in which they are found in the Bible itself. But this book will serve you best if you read it first in its entirety before using it during an actual encounter with Jehovah's Witnesses.

1

What Jehovah's Witnesses Believe

In some areas, of course, Jehovah's Witnesses believe much the same as orthodox Christians—for example, their rejection, as sin, of sex outside marriage; their acceptance of the Bible's creation account, as opposed to the evolution theory; and their belief that the Bible is the inspired Word of God. But, in many other areas, their doctrines set them apart and mark them as a pseudo-Christian cult—especially the sect's teachings on the following matters (for related Scripture texts and further details, see Subject Index):

Armageddon: God will soon wage war against mankind, destroying everyone on earth except Jehovah's Witnesses. The churches of Christendom, they say, will be the first to be destroyed.

Birthdays: Celebrating a birthday in any manner is strictly forbidden. Even sending a birthday card can bring swift action against the offender by an official "judicial committee." The punishment is "disfellowshiping" (see below).

Blood Transfusions: In actual practice, JW's view

accepting a blood transfusion as a sin more serious than theft or adultery. Thieves and adulterers are more quickly forgiven by Watchtower judicial committees than individuals found guilty of taking blood. A Witness must refuse blood in all circumstances, even when this is certain to result in death. The organization also requires adults to refuse transfusions for their minor children.

Christianity: Except for a few scattered individuals who kept the faith, true Christianity vanished from the face of the earth shortly after the death of the twelve apostles—according to Jehovah's Witnesses. It was not restored until Charles Taze Russell set up the Watchtower organization in the late 1870s. When Christ returned invisibly in 1914, he found Russell's group doing the work of the "faithful and wise servant" (Matt. 24:45) and appointed them over all his belongings. All other churches and professed Christians are actually tools of the devil.

Christ's Return: The Lord returned invisibly in the year 1914 and has been present ever since, ruling as King on earth through the Watchtower Society. References to the second "coming" are rendered as "presence" in the Jehovah's Witness Bible. The generation of people who witnessed Christ's invisible return in 1914 will not pass away before Armageddon comes (see Matt. 24:34)

Chronology: Jehovah's Witnesses believe that God has a precise timetable for all past and future events, tied together by simple mathematical formulae and revealed to mankind through the Watchtower Society. The seven "days" of the Genesis creation account were each seven thousand years long, for a total "week" of forty-nine thousand years. God created Adam in the year 4026 B.C. His creation of Eve a short time later marked the end of the Sixth Creative Day and the beginning of the Seventh. Therefore, we are now approximately 6,000 years into that 7,000-year period—which means that Armageddon will soon put an end to 6,000 years of human toil, making way for a Sabbath-like thousand-year reign of Christ. On the basis of this chronology, the JW organization has promulgated a number of specific end-times prophecies.

Cross: According to Jehovah's Witnesses, the cross is a pagan religious symbol adopted by the church when Satan, the devil, took control of ecclesiastical authority. It had nothing to do with Christ's death, since JW's maintain that he was nailed to a straight upright pole without a crossbeam. Witnesses abhor the cross, and new converts are expected to destroy any crosses they may have, rather than simply dispose of them.

Deity: The Father alone is God, and true worshipers must call him by the name *Jehovah*. Witnesses are taught that Jesus Christ was merely a manifestation of Michael the archangel in human form—not God, but a mere created being. The Holy Spirit is presented as neither God nor a person but, rather, as an "active force."

Disfellowshiping: This is the punishment for any infraction of Watchtower organizational regulations. It consists of a public decree, announced to the audience at a Kingdom Hall meeting and prohibiting all association or fellowship with the offender. Other Witnesses are forbidden even to say "Hello" if they encounter the offender on the street. The only exceptions are that family members may conduct "necessary business" with a disfellowshiped person, and elders may speak to him if he approaches them repentantly to seek reinstatement.

Heaven: Only 144,000 individuals go to heaven. This "little flock" began with the twelve apostles, and the number was filled by the year 1935. Approximately 9,000 elderly JW's are the only remaining ones on earth today who will go to heaven, with the rest of the Jehovah's Witnesses hoping to live on earth forever.

Hell: Following the lead of its founder, Charles T. Russell, the Watchtower Society still teaches that *hades* is merely the grave, that the fire of *Gehenna* instantly disintegrates its victims into nothingness, and that there is no conscious existence for the dead until the time of their bodily resurrection.

Holidays: Celebration of any "worldly holiday" is strictly forbidden for Jehovah's Witnesses. This prohibition applies to U.S. presidents' birthdays, Valentine's Day, Memorial Day, Christmas, Easter, New Year's Day, Thanksgiving, Good Friday, and so on— even Mother's Day and Father's Day! Even if a "pagan origin" cannot be researched as the basis for banning a particular observance, the simple fact that "worldly people" celebrate it is sufficient reason for the JW's *not* to celebrate it.

Holy Spirit: The Holy Spirit is neither God nor a person, according to Watchtower teaching. "It" is simply an impersonal "active force" that God uses in doing his will.

Hope: JW's believe that God stopped calling Christians to a heavenly hope back in the year 1935. Since then, he has been offering people the opportunity to live forever on this earth. ("Millions now living will never die!" is a familiar Jehovah's Witness slogan.) God will destroy everyone else on the planet, leaving only Jehovah's Witnesses, and he will restore a Garden-of-Eden paradise for them worldwide.

Jesus Christ: In Watchtower theology, Jesus Christ is a mere angel—the first one that God created when he started creating angels. Witnesses identify Christ as Michael the archangel, although they call Jesus "the Son of God"—because "the first spirit person God made was like a firstborn son to him" (1982 Watchtower booklet, *Enjoy Life on Earth Forever!*, p. 14). They also call him "a god," and translate John 1:1 accordingly in their Bible.

Organization: Witnesses believe that God set up the Watchtower organization as his channel of communication to gather together those of mankind who will be saved. As the visible agency of the kingdom of God on earth, this organization exercises full governmental authority over believers—it promulgates laws, puts violators on trial, operates Kingdom schools, and so on—parallel to the secular government. If there is a conflict between the two, the organization is to be obeyed, rather than the secular rulers. (In the Witnesses' minds, they are "obeying God rather than men," Acts 5:29.)

Resurrection: Concerning Christ, JW's believe that he became nonexistent when he died and that he was raised three days later as a "spirit"—an angel. They deny his bodily resurrection. Going along with their teaching that Christ returned invisibly in 1914, Witnesses believe that he raised dead Christians to spirit life shortly thereafter, and that the rest of the human dead will be raised bodily during the thousand-year reign of God's kingdom.

Salvation: Although giving lip service to salvation through faith in Christ, Witnesses actually believe that salvation is impossible apart from full obedience to the Watchtower Society and vigorous participation in its prescribed works program. Even individual JW's who are not sufficiently zealous for the organization

15

may not survive Armageddon, and those who do make their way into the earthly paradise must maintain good works throughout Christ's thousand-year reign before they can be sealed for life.

2

The Bible That Jehovah's Witnesses Use

Christians embarking on discussions with Jehovah's Witnesses should be aware that the so-called Bible the Witnesses use contains a number of changes introduced to the text for the sole purpose of supporting Watchtower doctrines.

The apostle Peter said concerning Paul's inspired letters that "There are some things in them hard to understand, which the ignorant and unstable twist to their own destruction, as they do the other scriptures" (2 Peter 3:16, RSV). Usually such "twisting" of Scripture is confined to interpretation—and that is what the Watchtower Society did for three-quarters of a century. They issued followers copies of the King James Version (or, later on, the American Standard Version, because it features the name "Jehovah" throughout the Old Testament), along with detailed instructions on how to make the Scriptures appear to teach that God outlawed vaccinations, that Abraham and the faithful prophets would be resurrected to this earth in 1925, that God inspired the Great Pyramid of Egypt, and so on. But there were some doctrines that were very difficult to derive from the King James Version and the

American Standard Version, no matter how much twisting was applied to the text.

So, during the 1950s, Watchtower leaders went beyond interpretation by producing their own version of the Bible, with hundreds of verses changed to fit Watchtower doctrines. And, their *New World Translation of the Holy Scriptures* continues to be rewritten every few years, with additional changes made to bring God's Word into closer agreement with what the organization teaches.

For example, instead of "the cross," the *New World Translation* substitutes "the torture stake"—to support the JW teaching that Jesus was nailed to an upright pole without a crossbeam. Instead of "the Holy Spirit," we find reference to "holy spirit" or "active force," in agreement with their denial of the deity and personality of the Holy Spirit. Christ speaks, not of his "coming" again, but of his "presence" (which Witnesses believe to be invisible).

The *New World Translation* systematically sets out to eliminate evidence for the deity of Christ. Instead of falling at Jesus' feet to "worship" him, people did "obeisance" to him. John 1:1 no longer says that "the Word was God"; here it reads, "the Word was a god." Jesus did not say, "Before Abraham was, I am." Rather, to avoid association with the "I AM" of Exodus 3:14, Jesus' statement becomes: "Before Abraham came into existence, I have been."

But the most widespread change in the Watchtower Bible is the insertion of the name *Jehovah* 237 times in the New Testament. Of course, it is appropriate for a translator to choose to use the divine name *Jehovah* or *Yahweh* in the Old Testament where the Tetragrammaton YHWH actually appears in the Hebrew text. But the Watchtower has gone beyond this by inserting the name *Jehovah* in the New Testament, where it does not appear in Greek manuscripts. One need only look at the word-for-word English that appears under the Greek text in the Society's own *Kingdom Interlinear Translation*, to see that the name *Jehovah* is not there in the Greek.

To find specific examples of the distortions outlined above, consult the Subject-Matter Index. Two outstanding cases that are useful in demonstrating the doctrinal bias of the JW Bible are Romans 14:8–9) (where the insertion of "Jehovah" produces a logical *non sequitur* in the English text) and Hebrews 1:6 (where early editions say the angels "worship" the Son of God, but later editions change this to "obeisance").

For a more detailed discussion, see *The Jehovah's Witnesses' New Testament* by Robert H. Countess (1982, Presbyterian and Reformed Publishing Co., 136 pages).

3

Verse-by-Verse Answers for JW's—Old Testament

Genesis

Genesis 1:1–2

> In the beginning God created the heavens and the earth. Now the earth proved to be formless and waste and there was darkness upon the surface of the watery deep; and God's *active force* was moving to and fro over the surface of the waters. (NWT, emphasis added)

Jehovah's Witnesses use this verse to attack Christian belief in the personality of the Holy Spirit. Most translations of verse 2 state that "the Spirit of God" was moving over the surface of the waters. But the Watchtower organization has taught its followers that the Holy Spirit is merely an impersonal force at God's disposal. To prove this point to anyone who will listen, Witnesses quote the verse as it appears in their own *New World Translation of the Holy Scriptures*. This is a situation in which individual JW's do not need to twist Scripture to fit the doctrines they have been taught—the verse comes already pre-twisted in their own Bible. (See chapter two.) In other texts, the Watchtower version speaks of "holy spirit," not capitalized and without the definite article in English.

Genesis 1:1–2

To answer the JW claim that the Holy Spirit is a mere impersonal force, emphasize to Witnesses that the Bible repeatedly refers to the Holy Spirit as having personal attributes. For example, even their own *New World Translation* reveals that the Spirit speaks (Acts 13:2), bears witness (John 15:26), says whatever he hears (John 16:13), feels hurt (Isa. 63:10), and so forth.

For further discussion on the Holy Spirit, see John 16:13; Acts 5:3–4; Romans 8:26–27; 1 Corinthians 6:19; and Subject Index.

Genesis 9:4

Only you shall not eat flesh with its life, that is, its blood (RSV).

This is the first of several Scripture verses that Jehovah's Witnesses use to argue in support of the Watchtower Society's ban on blood transfusions. The organization teaches that a blood transfusion is the same as eating blood, because it resembles intravenous feeding. The Society accordingly prohibits blood transfusions for its followers. A Witness who accepts a transfusion can expect to be summoned before a judicial committee to be put on trial behind closed doors for violation of "God's law." The punishment, if found guilty, is "disfellowshiping," whereby the individual is shunned by family and friends who are forbidden even to greet the offender.

Jehovah's Witnesses feel very strongly about this issue. They will die rather than accept a transfusion to replace blood lost in an operation or accident. And they follow this same course with respect to their minor children. Most Witnesses carry a signed card in their wallet or purse, stating their refusal to accept blood and instructing emergency medical personnel not to administer a transfusion if the Witness is found unconscious. The card is a legal document, signed by the JW and countersigned by two others.

JW's recognize that they are unique among religious

people in their stand on blood transfusions, although it does not occur to them that this very fact shows that the doctrine does not really derive from the Bible. No one else who attempts to follow the Bible as a guide in life has come up with a ban on transfusions—and even the Watchtower organization did not promulgate the doctrine until 1944.

Most Jehovah's Witnesses are unaware that their leaders have had a history of introducing other medical prohibitions and then later changing their mind. In 1967, for example, they prohibited organ transplants. Followers were expected to choose blindness rather than accept a cornea transplant, or to die rather than submit to a kidney transplant. But then, in 1980, the leaders reversed the teaching and allowed transplants once again (see *The Watchtower,* 11/15/67, pp. 702–704; *Awake!* 6/8/68, p. 21; and *The Watchtower,* 3/15/80, p. 31). In addition, between the years 1931 and 1952, JW's had to refuse vaccinations for themselves and their children because the organization taught them: "Vaccination is a direct violation of the everlasting covenant that God made . . ." (*The Golden Age,* 2/4/31, p. 293).

Even though Witnesses will attempt to quote Scripture to support their position on blood transfusions, the real reason for their stand is blind obedience to the Watchtower Society. If the organization lifted its prohibition tomorrow, Witnesses would freely accept transfusions—just as they did an about-face when the vaccination ban was lifted in 1952 and when the ban on organ transplants was rescinded in 1980.

See also the discussions of Leviticus 7:26–27 and Acts 15:28–29.

Genesis 18:1–2

> Yahweh appeared to him. . . . . He looked up, and there he saw three men. . . . (JB)

23

Jehovah's Witnesses believe that it is impossible for the one true God to exist as three persons: Father, Son, and Holy Spirit. Yet, the Bible, in Genesis 18 and 19, shows God appearing to Abraham as three men. This account can be used to help JW's see that even the impossible (from a human viewpoint) is possible with God. Discuss it with them, as suggested here:

In the Watchtower Society's own *New World Translation,* at Genesis 18:1-2, God appears to Abraham as three men (or angels). Abraham addresses the three as "Jehovah" (v. 3). When the three men respond, the episode is described interchangeably as "they" speaking (v. 9) and "Jehovah" speaking (v. 13). When two of the three men depart to visit Lot in Sodom, Abraham continues to call the remaining one "Jehovah," but Lot addresses the other two as "Jehovah" (Gen. 18:22, 30 and 19:1, 18).

By itself, this account does not *prove* the Trinity doctrine. But, at the very least, it demonstrates that it is possible for God to manifest himself as three-in-one. The fact that this concept is beyond the full grasp of human intellect should not cause Jehovah's Witnesses to rule it out. As the apostle Paul wrote: ". . . we can see and understand only a little about God now, as if we were peering at his reflection in a poor mirror; but someday we are going to see him in his completeness, face to face. Now all that I know is hazy and blurred, but then I will see everything clearly, just as clearly as God sees into my heart right now" (1 Cor. 13:12, LB).

The discussion above may help a Jehovah's Witness to reconsider the concept of one God in three persons. For further help, see also Isaiah 9:6; John 1:1; John 16:13; 1 Corinthians 6:19; 1 Corinthians 8:6; Colossians 2:9; and Revelation 1:7-8.

Genesis 40:20-22

> And it came to pass the third day, which was Pharaoh's birthday, that he made a feast unto all his servants. . . . But he hanged the chief baker. . . . (KJV)

The Watchtower organization has prohibited birthday celebrations among its adherents, using Genesis 40:20–22 as a key part of the "scriptural basis" for this ruling. Their thought is that the word *birthday* appears in the Bible only in reference to Pharaoh of Egypt (as above) and King Herod of Galilee (Matt. 14:6 and Mark 6:21). Both of them were pagans, and both men had someone put to death in connection with the celebration. Since no men of faith are recorded in the Bible as having celebrated their birthdays, but only wicked men—so the Watchtower reasoning goes— Jehovah's Witnesses of today must not be allowed to celebrate birthdays either.

It is worth noting that, as with other teachings, it is not left up to the individual Witness to read the Bible and come up with this conclusion. Rather, the sect's secretive governing body has promulgated this official interpretation and uses its disciplinary procedures to enforce the policy on all Witnesses. For example, one elderly JW of our acquaintance in Massachusetts decided that he would send a birthday card to his non-Witness son, but his wife reported it to the local elders. They summoned him before a closed-door judicial-committee meeting and put him on trial for this offense. The seventy-year-old gentleman challenged them to show him one Scripture verse prohibiting sending a birthday card, but the committee went ahead and disfellowshiped him on the basis of the Watchtower Society's ruling. His Witness relatives now refuse him admittance to their home, and Witnesses who encounter him on the street turn away without even saying hello.

In refuting the Watchtower's so-called scriptural basis for banning birthday celebrations, you can point out that Pharaoh and King Herod were arbitrary rulers and violent men; such monarchs were accustomed to executing people on all sorts of occasions, not just on their birthdays. Moreover, a person sending a birthday card, or a parent providing a cake with candles at a children's party, can hardly be accused of following the pattern of those murderous men.

Although the actual word *birthday* appears only in connection with Pharaoh and Herod in most translations, the Bible does contain reference to such celebrations in godly families:

In Job 1:4, it says of the patriarch Job's family, "And his sons went and held a banquet at the house of each one *on his own day;* and they sent and invited their three sisters to eat and drink with them" (NWT, italics added). That "his own day" refers to each one's birthday becomes clear when we read further: "It was after this that Job opened his mouth and began to call down evil upon *his day.* Job now answered and said: 'Let *the day* perish *on which I came to be born* . . .' " (Job 3:1–3, NWT, italics added). The Living Bible's paraphrase of Job 1:4–5 expresses this thought: "Every year when each of Job's sons had a birthday, he invited his brothers and sisters to his home for a celebration. On these occasions they would eat and drink with great merriment. When these birthday parties ended. . . ."

Even the Watchtower Society's own translation reveals that the birth of John the Baptist was celebrated, when it records this angelic announcement: "And you will have joy and great gladness, and many will rejoice over his birth" (Luke 1:14, NWT).

If the birth of John the Baptist was an occasion for rejoicing and if faithful Job's children celebrated their birthdays, the fact that Pharaoh and Herod also celebrated theirs cannot logically be used as a basis for banning birthday parties among Bible believers today.

Exodus

Exodus 3:14

God said to Moses, "I AM WHO I AM." And he said, "Say this to the people of Israel, 'I AM has sent me to you.' " (RSV)

Christians universally recognize that Jesus Christ was claiming to be the Deity when he referred to himself as the I AM: "The Jews then said to him, 'You are not yet fifty years old, and have you seen Abraham?' Jesus said to them, 'Truly, truly, I say to you, before Abraham was, I am'" (John 8:57–58, RSV). Even Jesus' enemies recognized what he was saying. The next verse tells us that, when they heard this, "they took up stones to throw at him . . ." (v. 59). The unbelieving Jews viewed Jesus' claim to be the I AM as blasphemy, a crime for which they wanted to stone him to death.

Jehovah's Witnesses, however, teach that Jesus Christ is really just Michael the archangel and that Christ never claimed to be God. So, to make Scripture agree with their doctrine, they change the reading of both verses in their Bible. The Watchtower Society's translation says, "This is what you are to say to the sons of Israel, 'I SHALL PROVE TO BE has sent me to you'" (Exod. 3:14, NWT), and "Most truly I say to you, Before Abraham came into existence, I have been" (John 8:58, NWT). So, in the JW Bible, Jesus' words appear to have no connection with Exodus 3:14.

But you do not have to be a Greek and Hebrew scholar to prove that the Watchtower Society has twisted these verses. Jehovah's Witnesses' own study Bibles prove that Jesus was claiming to be the I AM. Their 1984 large-print *New World Translation of the Holy Scriptures with References* has a footnote on Exodus 3:14, admitting that the Hebrew would be rendered into Greek as *"Ego eimi"*—*"I am."* And their 1985 *Kingdom Interlinear Translation of the Greek Scriptures* reveals that Jesus' words at John 8:58 are the same: *"ego eimi"* (footnote), *"I am"* (interlinear text).

Exodus 3:15

Then God said once more to Moses: "This is what you are to say to the sons of Israel, 'Jehovah the God of your forefathers, the God of Abraham, the God of Isaac and the God of Jacob, has sent me to you.' This is my name to time indefinite, and this is the memorial of me to generation after generation." (NWT)

Jehovah's Witnesses use this verse to argue that they are the only true worshipers of God, because they are the only ones who still call God by his name—Jehovah. The above verse, they insist, is God's command to call him by that sacred name "to time indefinite," or forever. In the eyes of JW's, Christians who pray to "God" or to "the Lord" are actually praying to the false god, Satan; the true God, Jehovah, does not hear prayers unless they are addressed to him by name. Therefore, Witnesses always use the name *Jehovah* in their prayers. In fact, they often repeat the name many times during a single prayer, as if God might forget that he is the one being addressed, or as if the Witness might forget to which God he was praying.

Although their own publications admit that "Jehovah" is an Anglicized misrendering and not the correct pronunciation of the original Hebrew Tetragrammaton YHWH, they insist upon using that pronunciation only, rather than the more correct name *Yahweh*. JW's never pray to "Yahweh."

A comparison of Exodus 3:15 with verse 14 shows that the name *Yahweh*, or *Jehovah*, has meaning: God is the self-existing Eternal One. He is much more than a name, and knowing him involves much more than using a name. Jesus showed that more than just a name is involved, when he said: "On that day many will say to me, 'Lord, Lord, did we not prophesy *in your name*, and cast out demons *in your name*, and do many mighty works *in your name?*' And then will I declare to them, 'I never knew you; depart from me, you evildoers' " (Matt. 7:22–23, RSV [italics added]).

Ask a Jehovah's Witness to examine with you the prayers of Jesus Christ. Point out that Jesus never started out his prayers by saying, "Jehovah God . . ."—as JW's do.

28

Rather, Jesus began his prayers by saying, "Father. . . ." (See Matt. 11:25, 26:39-42; Mark 14:36; Luke 10:21, 22:42, 23:34, 46; John 11:41, 12:27-28, 17:1-26.) And, when teaching his disciples how to pray, Jesus instructed them to address "Our Father . . ." (Matt. 6:9; Luke 11:2). Christians, then, are to have an intimate relationship with God as his children who call out to him, "Abba! Father!" (Rom. 8:15; Gal. 4:6).

And, as to the importance of names, the Holy Spirit inspired Peter to stress ". . . the name of Jesus Christ . . . . there is no other name under heaven given among men by which we must be saved" (Acts 4:10-12, RSV). Moreover, *Jesus* is "the name which is above every name, that at the name of Jesus every knee should bow, in heaven and on earth and under the earth, and every tongue confess that Jesus Christ is Lord, to the glory of God the Father" (Phil. 2:9-11, RSV).

See also the discussions on Psalm 83:18 and Isaiah 43:10 in this chapter.

Leviticus 7:26—27

And you must not eat any blood in any places where you dwell, whether that of fowl or that of beast. Any soul who eats any blood, that soul must be cut off from his people. (NWT)

This text is frequently quoted in support of the Watchtower Society's ban on blood transfusions. Even though the verse specifically forbade Israelites to *eat* the blood of fowl or beast, Jehovah's Witnesses stretch its meaning to include medical administration of human blood to save life—a thought obviously not intended when Moses recorded God's words. Leviticus discusses at great length the divinely ordained arrangements for animal sacrifice by the Jewish priesthood, and blood played a major role in those sacrifices as a foreshadow of the precious blood of our Savior, the Lamb of God, Jesus Christ. Any attempt to read these verses as a prophetic ruling on the pros and cons of modern medical procedures totally ignores the context of the passage.

When discussing Leviticus 7:26–27 with Jehovah's Witnesses, you might bring up the fact that Orthodox Jews of today, who still scrupulously observe the regulations for kosher butchering and bleeding of meat, have no religious objection to blood transfusions. Therefore, the original Hebrew text does not even hint at the interpretation that the Watchtower imposes upon it.

If a Jehovah's Witness still insists that he must refuse blood transfusions on account of Leviticus 7:26–27, the next move would be to show him Leviticus 3:17, which says: "You must not eat any fat or any blood at all" (NWT). Ask him to explain why Watchtower leaders tell him to refuse blood transfusions but allow him to eat fat. Are they not simply pulling words out of context from Jewish dietary laws?

See also the discussions of Genesis 9:4 and Acts 15:28–29.

Deuteronomy 18:20—22

"However, the prophet who presumes to speak in my name a word that I have not commanded him to speak or who speaks in the name of other gods, that prophet must die. And in case you should say in your heart: 'How shall we know the word that Jehovah has not spoken?' when the prophet speaks in the name of Jehovah and the word does not occur or come true, that is the word that Jehovah did not speak. With presumptuousness the prophet spoke it. You must not get frightened at him." (NWT).

The Watchtower organization identifies itself as "The Prophet," saying: "This 'prophet' was not one man, but was a body of men and women. It was the small group of footstep followers of Jesus Christ, known at that time as International Bible Students. Today they are known as

Jehovah's Christian witnesses. They are still proclaiming a warning . . ." (*The Watchtower,* 4/1/72, p. 197). The added claim is made that: "Unless we are in touch with this channel of communication that God is using, we will not progress along the road to life, no matter how much Bible reading we do" (*The Watchtower,* 12/1/81, p. 27).

Are these claims true? Is the Watchtower organization really *the* Prophet, the channel of communication from God? Or, is it a false prophet, fitting the description of Deuteronomy 18:20–22? The test is simple: Step #1—We know the organization "spoke in the name of Jehovah"; Step #2—We must determine whether or not the prophecies actually did occur or come true. Let's examine the facts:

Throughout half of its hundred-year history, the Watchtower Society taught the belief of its founder and first president, Charles Taze Russell, that the Great Pyramid of Egypt was "inspired" of God—just like the Bible (see the Watchtower's book *Thy Kingdom Come,* 1903 edition, p. 362). The Society's publications translated inches of pyramid measurements into calendar years, in attempts to foretell future events. Thus, they predicted that the Battle of Armageddon "will end in A.D. 1914 with the complete overthrow of earth's present rulership" (*The Time Is at Hand,* 1904 edition, p. 101). Obviously, this did not occur or come true.

Still determined to act as a prophet, the Watchtower Society went on to predict an earthly resurrection for the year 1925: "They are to be resurrected as perfect men and constitute the princes or rulers in the earth, according to his promise. . . . Therefore we may confidently expect that 1925 will mark the return of Abraham, Isaac, Jacob and the faithful prophets of old" (Watchtower's book *Millions Now Living Will Never Die,* 1920, pp. 89–90). Did this occur or come true? No!

More recently, the organization misled millions into believing that "the end" would come in 1975. They asked:

31

"Why Are You Looking Forward to 1975?" (title of article in *The Watchtower,* 8/15/68, p. 494):

> Are we to assume from this study that the battle of Armageddon will be all over by the autumn of 1975, and the long-looked-for thousand-year reign of Christ will begin by then? Possibly, but we wait to see how closely the seventh thousand-year period of man's existence coincides with the sabbathlike thousand-year reign of Christ. If these two periods run parallel with each other as to the calendar year, it will not be by mere chance or accident but will be according to Jehovah's loving and timely purposes. . . . It may involve only a difference of weeks or months, not years [p. 499].

Certainly, by now, enough weeks, months, and years have passed to prove that this prophecy concerning 1975 did not occur or come true.

A JW may try to defend the Watchtower Society, saying that those false prophecies were all "mistakes" and that the organization has learned from these mistakes and no longer makes prophetic statements about when the end will come. In that case, ask the Witness to take out a copy of his latest *Awake!* magazine. Inside the front cover, on the page listing the contents of the magazine, there is a statement of purpose telling why *Awake!* is published. Ask the Witness to read it. As of this writing (1986), each issue still says: "Most importantly, this magazine builds confidence in the Creator's promise of a peaceful and secure New Order before the generation that saw the events of 1914 passes away." Another prophecy! (See our discussion of Matt. 24:34 in the next chapter.)

The facts are inescapable: The Watchtower Society spoke as a prophet in the name of God, and what was prophesied did not come true. What does this mean for the individual Jehovah's Witness? Invite one to read what God's Word says about false prophets—and then ask what God would have him or her do. The Bible contains these warnings from Jesus Christ: "Beware of false prophets, who come to you in sheep's clothing but inwardly are ravenous wolves." "For false Christs and false prophets will arise . . ." (Matt. 7:15, and 24:24, RSV). And the strong words quoted above from Deuteronomy 18:20–22, besides expressing God's judgment that the false prophet "must die," also tell listeners, "You must not get frightened at him." Rather than remain fearfully obedient to Watchtower leaders, the individual Jehovah's Witness who recognizes the organization as a false prophet should quit following it and start following the true Prophet, Jesus Christ.

Psalms

Psalm 37:9, 11, 29

> For evildoers themselves will be cut off, But those hoping in Jehovah are the ones that will possess the earth. . . . But the meek ones themselves will possess the earth. . . . The righteous themselves will possess the earth, And they will reside forever upon it. (NWT)

Jehovah's Witnesses commonly turn to these verses in their door-to-door preaching to introduce listeners to the hope of life in an earthly paradise, rather than going to heaven. According to the Watchtower Society, the opportunity to go to heaven ended in the year 1935. Instead, Witnesses look forward to surviving the destruction of the rest of mankind at Armageddon and living forever on earth.

When read in context, however, the verses quoted from Psalm 37 paint a different picture. The psalm is not foretelling a future time when God will remove the wicked and turn control of the earth over to good people. Rather, the psalmist was inspired to tell his fellow Israelites what they could expect to see in their own lifetime—good men

33

would prosper under God's blessing, while wicked men would fare badly. For example, in verse 25, David writes, "A young man I used to be, I have also grown old, And yet I have not seen anyone righteous left entirely, Nor his offspring looking for bread" (NWT). He is speaking of events during his own lifetime. And in verse 37, he adds, "Watch the blameless one and keep the upright one in sight, For the future of that man will be peaceful." Again, the context concerns the immediate benefits of good conduct. The psalm contains no indication that it should be taken as a prophetic statement about the end of the world.

Other verses used by Jehovah's Witnesses to teach an earthly hope, instead of heaven, include Psalm 115:16, John 10:16, and Revelation 7:9. See discussions elsewhere in this book.

Psalm 83:18

> That men may know that thou, whose name alone is JEHO-VAH, art the most high over all the earth. (KJV)

This is one of the few verses that Jehovah's Witnesses like to quote from versions other than their own slanted *New World Translation*. In particular, they like to quote Psalm 83:18 from the King James Version, because the name *JEHOVAH* appears there in all capital letters.

Many Witnesses have noted in the back of their Bibles a list of the four places where *JEHOVAH* can be found in the King James Version: Exodus 6:3, Psalm 83:18, Isaiah 12:2, and Isaiah 26:4. In their door-to-door preaching they will ask an unsuspecting householder, "Do you have your own Bible handy?" and then focus attention on one of those verses. Caught off guard by finding *JEHOVAH* in their own Bible where the Witnesses said it would be, some people become impressed with their knowledge and allow the Witnesses into the home to teach them more.

Of course, the Jehovah's Witnesses' use of the Bible in

this way—to demonstrate their superior knowledge and their claim to "know God by name"—is just a clever trick. There are other cultic and occultic groups that use transliterations of Hebrew names for God, with similar effect on the uninitiated. But the fact of the matter is that using a name for God does not guarantee that the user knows God or is approved by him.

For example, when sinner Eve gave birth to her first son after being driven out from the Garden of Eden, she exclaimed, "I have produced a man with the aid of Jehovah" (Gen. 4:1, NWT). Her use of God's name did not in any way prove that she had his approval.

To show Jehovah's Witnesses that their use of the name *Jehovah* does not guarantee that they belong to him, you may wish to quote Jesus' words in Matthew 7:22–23: "Many will say to me in that day, Lord, Lord, have we not prophesied *in thy name?* and *in thy name* have cast out devils? and *in thy name* done many wonderful works? And then will I profess unto them, I never knew you: depart from me, ye that work iniquity" (KJV, italics added).

See also the discussions on Exodus 3:15 and Isaiah 43:10.

Psalm 110:1

> The LORD said unto my Lord, Sit thou at my right hand, until I make thine enemies thy footstool. (KJV)

Jehovah's Witnesses calling at a home may invite the householder to get his own Bible and open it to Psalm 110:1. Then they will ask him to read the verse. The householder reads that "the LORD said unto my Lord . . ." and is immediately confused. Then the Witnesses open their *New World Translation* and read the same verse: "The utterance of Jehovah to my Lord is. . . ." They go on to argue (1) that the *New World Translation* is a superior Bible to use, because it does not have the Lord talking to himself; and (2) that the Lord Jesus must be a mere cre-

35

ated being, since Jehovah God is addressing a person distinct from himself.

To answer the first argument, it is only necessary to look at the text more closely. It does not say that "the Lord" was talking to "the Lord." Most translations render the Hebrew tetragrammaton YHWH as "the LORD" (all capital letters), who is talking to the psalmist's "Lord" (both capital and small letters), the Messiah. If confusion results, the problem is not with the translation but rather with a lack of biblical education on the part of the reader. Knowledgeable Christians who read this verse will grasp that God the Father is speaking to the Son.

The second Witness argument—that Jesus cannot *be* God because "the LORD" spoke to him—is also a faulty one. The New Testament records many conversations between Jesus and the Father, but this does not disprove the deity of Christ. The Bible reveals that the Father is God (John 6:27, etc.) and that the Son is God (Isa. 9:6, John 20:28, etc.), yet there is only one God (1 Cor. 8:4). Although this appears to contradict everyday human logic, are we right to assume that God must fit into the logical patterns with which we are familiar in the world around us? He is from the realms above; we are from the realms below. His ways are beyond our full understanding.

In explaining to Witnesses the fact that Psalm 110 shows God, the Father in heaven, talking to the Son (also God) upon the earth, it may help to invite them to turn to Genesis 18 and 19 in their own *New World Translation*. There it says that "Jehovah appeared to him" [Abraham] as "three men" or angels (18:1–2). Abraham addressed the three as "Jehovah" (18:3). Two of them left Abraham and went toward the city of Sodom, but Abraham continued to address the remaining individual as "Jehovah" (18:22, 19:1). When the other two reached Sodom and spoke with Abraham's relative Lot, he addressed the two of them as "Jehovah" (19:18). And, when the city of Sodom was destroyed, the *New World Translation* says at Genesis 19:24: "Then

Jehovah made it rain sulphur and fire from Jehovah, from the heavens. . . ." So, unless the Witnesses want to claim that there is more than one Jehovah, they will have to admit that God can be in more than one place at the same time, and that he can hold simultaneous conversations with different people in different places. This should make it easier for them to grasp that the Father can talk to the Son, without calling into question the deity of Christ.

Psalm 115:16

The heaven, even the heavens, are the LORD's: but the earth hath he given to the children of men. (KJV)

Jehovah's Witnesses often quote this verse to "prove" that man's destiny is life on earth, not in heaven. The Watchtower Society teaches that only a limited number of 144,000 would be eligible for heavenly life, and that this number was reached by the year 1935. Since then, the sect has been teaching new converts to look forward to everlasting life on an earth restored to paradise conditions. (See the discussion of Rev. 7:9, for consideration of the 1935 date.)

This is one of many areas in which the Watchtower organization turns mainly to the Old Testament and leads its members back into a twisted form of Judaism, denying essential features of the New Covenant mediated by Jesus Christ. (Other examples of Judaizing include focusing on the Hebrew name *Jehovah;* denying the deity of Christ; inculcating a salvation-through-works mentality; strict legalism; and so on.) The best way to answer the Witnesses on this point is to turn them to the New Testament and show them the "heavenly calling" (Heb. 3:1) given by the Savior to all who would follow him.

For example, Jesus tells us: "In my Father's house are many mansions: if it were not so, I would have told you. I go to prepare a place for you. And if I go and prepare a place for you, I will come again, and receive you unto myself; that where I am, there ye may be also" (John 14:2-3, KJV). When Jesus prayed to the Father "that they also, whom thou has given me, be with me where I am; that they may behold my glory," he was praying not only for his original disciples, "but for them also which shall believe on me through their word" (John 17:20, 24, KJV). Ask the Witnesses if they have believed on Christ through the word of the apostles. If they can truly answer *yes,* then they are included in Christ's prayer that all future believers would end up with him in heaven.

See also the discussions of Psalm 37:9, 11, 29; John 10:16; Revelation 7:9.

Psalm 146:3-4

> Put not your trust in princes, in a son of man, in whom there is no help. When his breath departs he returns to his earth; on that very day his plans perish. (RSV)

In the King James Version, verse 4 ends with the expression "in that very day his thoughts perish," and the Watchtower's *New World Translation* similarly says, "In that day his thoughts do perish." Jehovah's Witnesses read the passage from either of these translations and use it to argue that there is no conscious existence after death— man's "thoughts" have perished, they point out.

However, is that the message that the writer of Psalm 146 meant to get across? Were those verses penned to instruct readers about the condition of the dead? Or do Jehovah's Witnesses extract from these words an idea beyond what the writer (and the divine Author) had in mind?

The lesson of Psalm 146 is that we should put our trust in God rather than in human leaders. Get the Jehovah's Witness to read the other verses with you to establish the real context. God is to be praised (v. 1-2). In contrast to man, God is a Helper who gives secure hope (v. 5), who created heaven and earth (v. 6), who brings justice for the oppressed (v. 7), who heals the sick (v. 8), who cares about the lowly ones (v. 9), and who is King forever (v. 10). Man, on the other hand, offers no real salvation (v. 3), because he himself dies and everything he intended to do dies with him (v. 4).

An actual example of the lesson of Psalm 146 is found in the death of President John F. Kennedy. He was a "prince" whom many people trusted to help them improve their lot in life. Yet, when he died, "all his thoughts did perish"—with him gone, his plans and programs soon collapsed. People who had put all their trust in him were disappointed. Their primary trust should have been in God, who offers real hope, justice, healing, and salvation— and who remains King forever.

When all of Psalm 146 is read in context, it becomes obvious that verse 4 does not deny conscious life after death. Jehovah's Witnesses misuse the verse by taking it out of context.

For further discussion of the condition of the dead, see Ecclesiastes 9:5; Ezekiel 18:4; and Luke 16:22-28.

Ecclesiastes 9:5

> For the living know that they will die, but the dead know nothing, and they have no more reward; but the memory of them is lost. (RSV)

This verse is frequently used by Jehovah's Witnesses in arguing that death brings annihilation—total nonexistence. To support the point even more conclusively, the Watchtower version reads this way: "For the living are conscious that they will die; but as for the dead, they are conscious of nothing at all . . ." (NWT). Now, if this verse is simply pulled out of context and quoted as authoritative, it appears to prove the JW's right. But taking such a passage out of context can be very dangerous.

A perfect illustration is the case of a certain transplant surgeon who, in speaking to reporters about a surgical procedure he was advocating, quoted Scripture: "Skin for skin, yea, all that a man hath will he give for his life." When I read the account in the newspaper, I was disturbed by his use of the verse, and, looking it up, I discovered that my suspicions were confirmed—he had quoted the devil! In context the verse in the King James Version says, "And *Satan* answered the Lord, and *said,* Skin for skin, yea, all that a man hath will he give for his life" (Job 2:4, italics added).

Besides giving God's viewpoint on matters, the Bible also relates many things said and done by others, some good and some not so good. It presents human viewpoints and even the devil's viewpoint, as noted above.

If we carefully study the Song of Solomon, found in most Bibles immediately after Ecclesiastes, we will discover that it is actually a running conversation involving at least three different speakers, although they are not clearly identified in the text. Could something similar be said about Ecclesiastes?

Scholars acknowledge that it is a very difficult book to understand. But, apparently, the inspired writer of Ecclesiastes is presenting a contrast of viewpoints: the secular, materialistic viewpoint *versus* the godly, spiritual one. The book reads like a running debate taking place in the mind of the writer. The godly viewpoint triumphs in the end, though, with the Ecclesiastes 12 admonition to "Remember now thy Creator in the days of thy youth. . . . Let us hear the conclusion of the whole matter: Fear God, and keep his commandments: for this is the whole duty of man" (vv. 1, 13, KJV).

But what of the parts that go before? The first ten verses of Ecclesiastes 9 appear to reflect the secular side of the struggle. Not only does the writer say in verse 5 that the dead know nothing, but he also adds that "they have no more *for ever* any share in all that is done under the sun" (v. 6, RSV, italics added). (Ask the Jehovah's Witness if he believes that the dead are gone *forever*. He will answer *no*, because he believes in a future resurrection to this earth under the sun.) Verse 2 (RSV) expresses the thought that "one fate comes to all, to the righteous and the wicked, to the good and the evil," an idea contradictory to all the rest of Scripture. (Ask the Witness if he believes that he will receive the same fate, whether he is righteous or wicked. His answer will have to be *no*.)

We can conclude that verse 5 is located in the midst of a section expressing the faithless, secular viewpoint—not God's.

What is God's viewpoint? Obviously, God knows whether or not the dead are conscious. And he has put into Scripture a number of references indicating the answer. Read those verses with the Jehovah's Witness, asking him what each one reveals about the condition of the dead:

> And when he opened the fifth seal, I saw underneath the altar the souls of those slaughtered because of the word of God and because of the witness work that they used to have. And they cried out with a loud voice, saying, "Until when, Sovereign Lord holy and true, are you refraining from judging and avenging our blood upon those who dwell on the earth?" And a white robe was given to each of them; and they were told to rest a little while longer, until the number was filled also of their fellow slaves and their brothers who were about to be killed as they also had been (Rev. 6:9–11, NWT).

> I am hard pressed between the two. My desire is to depart and be with Christ, for that is far better. But to remain in the flesh is more necessary on your account (Phil. 1:23–24, RSV).

> [Jesus said:] "The poor man died and was carried by the angels to Abraham's bosom. The rich man also died and was buried; and in Hades, being in torment, he lifted up his eyes. . . ." (Luke 16:22–23, RSV).

41

Isaiah 9:6

See also our discussions of Psalm 37:9, 11, 29; Psalm 146:3-4; Ezekiel 18:4; and Luke 16:22-28.

Isaiah

Isaiah 9:6

> For unto us a child is born, unto us a son is given: and the government shall be upon his shoulder: and his name shall be called Wonderful, Counsellor, The mighty God, The everlasting Father, The Prince of Peace (KJV)

Jehovah's Witnesses do not question that this verse speaks prophetically of Jesus Christ, identifying him as the "Mighty God" (NWT). But they believe that the Son is merely "a god"—one of the "many 'gods' and many 'lords' " (1 Cor. 8:5, NWT)—just as Satan, the devil, is called "the god of this system of things" (2 Cor. 4:4, NWT). They see Jesus Christ as a created being, an angel. According to Watchtower theology, he is definitely not Almighty God Jehovah.

The Witnesses actually have two gods, a big one and a little one: an "Almighty God," Jehovah—and a "mighty god," Jesus Christ. In practice, though, Jehovah gets all the worship, and Jesus is only called "a god" by way of concession.

You might start out by asking the Witnesses if they believe there is only one True God. They will answer "yes." Ask them who he is, and they will answer "Jehovah." Then have them read Isaiah 9:6, and ask them who is the Mighty God spoken of there—the "child born to us . . . a son given to us" (NWT). They will admit that Jesus is the Mighty God. Now ask them if Jesus is the one True God. They will answer "no!"—that Jesus is merely "a god." At this juncture, point out to them that their theology leads to one of two conclusions: either (1) not being the True God, Jesus would have to be a *false* god, or (2) they have *two* True Gods.

Now turn to the Bible to show the Jehovah's Witnesses that the Mighty God and the Almighty God are the same. You can do this in two steps. First, show that the risen Christ is not just mighty, but Almighty; and second, show that Almighty God Jehovah is also called the Mighty God.

First: Have the Witness read, at Hebrews 1:3, that Jesus Christ is "upholding the universe by his word of power" (RSV). How could anyone be more almighty than that? Then turn to Matthew 28:18 and show that Jesus Christ has "all authority" (NWT) or "all power . . . in heaven and in earth" (KJV). By definition, this is what the word *almighty* means. Therefore, Jesus Christ is almighty.

Second: Ask the Witness: "Since Isaiah was a Jew and therefore believed in only one God—Jehovah—who did Isaiah understand the Mighty God to be?" Certainly, Isaiah understood the Mighty God to be Jehovah. Next, invite the Witness to read Isaiah 10:20–21 in his own Watchtower Bible: ". . . those remaining over of Israel . . . will certainly support themselves upon Jehovah, the Holy One of Israel, in trueness. A mere remnant will return, the remnant of Jacob, to the Mighty God." Yes, the inspired Word penned through Isaiah calls *Jehovah* "the Mighty God."

Finally, to reinforce the point, ask the Witness to turn to Jeremiah 32:18 in his own *New World Translation*. But, before he reads it, remind him that the Watchtower organization teaches that the Mighty God and the Almighty God are different—Jesus being the Mighty one and Jehovah the Almighty one. Then have the Witness read what Jeremiah wrote about "the true God, the great One, the *mighty* One, Jehovah of armies being his name . . ." (Jer. 32:18, NWT, italics added). So, since Jesus is *the* Mighty God, and Jehovah is *the* Mighty God, who must Jesus be? (Let the JW reach the inescapable conclusion in his own mind that Jesus *is* Jehovah.)

See also our consideration of John 1:1; John 20:28; and Revelation 1:7–8.

43

Isaiah 43:10

"You are my witnesses," is the utterance of Jehovah. . . . (NWT)

Jehovah's Witnesses believe that they alone, out of all the religious groups on earth, are God's people, chosen by God and named as his witnesses. They love to point an accusing finger at Lutherans, Mennonites, and other denominations, as followers of men they are named after— Luther, Menno, and so on—while only JW's are followers of Jehovah God.

Actually, though, Jehovah's Witnesses were widely known as "Russellites" (after the Watchtower Society's founder, Charles Taze Russell), from the beginning of the movement in the 1870s, until the year 1931. The new name, Jehovah's Witnesses, was officially adopted by a resolution passed at their Columbus, Ohio, convention in 1931—primarily to distinguish them from other groups that also followed Russell.

But the simplistic idea that God singles out JW's from among all professing Christians, and considers them alone as his people because they use the name *Jehovah's Witnesses,* is just as preposterous as the view that any group calling itself "the Church of Christ" or "the Church of God" must actually be what its name implies—to the exclusion of all others.

Jesus showed that more is involved than just a name, when he said:

"Not every one who says to me, 'Lord, Lord,' shall enter the kingdom of heaven, but he who does the will of my Father who is in heaven. On that day many will say to me, 'Lord, Lord, did we not prophesy *in your name,* and cast out demons *in your name,* and do many mighty works *in your name?*' And then will I declare to them, 'I never knew you; depart from me, you evildoers.' " (Matt. 7:21–23, RSV, italics added)

By seeking to identify themselves with the ancient Hebrew name of God, rather than with the name of Jesus Christ, Jehovah's Witnesses are unconsciously revealing themselves as modern Judaizers. Jesus said, "You will be *My* witnesses" (Acts 1:8, MLB, italics added). And history records that "the disciples were called *Christians*" (Acts 11:26, KJV, italics added).

Ezekiel 18:4

> Behold, all souls are mine; as the soul of the father, so also the soul of the son is mine: the soul that sinneth, it shall die.
> (KJV)

"So," says the Jehovah's Witness, "the soul dies. This verse proves that there is no conscious life after death." Does it? Not at all! First, look at the context. What is the writer talking about? The Israelites were grumbling against God, quoting a proverb that said: "The fathers have eaten sour grapes, and the children's teeth are set on edge" (v. 2)—they were complaining that punishment for what a father did fell upon his offspring. Verse 4 is God's reply: The one who sins is the one who will die. The Living Bible's paraphrase renders it, accordingly: "For all souls are mine to judge—fathers and sons alike—and my rule is this: It is for a man's own sins that he will die." So, the context reveals that the inspired Word was not speaking here about the condition of the dead.

The word *soul* is used in many different senses throughout Scripture. It sometimes refers to a person's life, sometimes to the person himself (as it does here at Ezekiel 18:4), and sometimes it refers to the inner part of man that lives on after death. Jehovah's Witnesses deny this last use of the word *soul*. They say that man totally ceases to exist at death, that when the body dies, there is nothing left. But there are many Scripture verses that prove them wrong:

For example, ask them to turn to Luke 12:4–5. Their own *New World Translation* says, ". . . Do not fear those who kill the body and after this are not able to do anything more. But I will indicate to you whom to fear: Fear him who after killing has authority to throw into Gehenna. Yes, I tell you, fear this One." Therefore, a man's body can be killed. He is dead. But something can be done to him *after* he is dead. He can then be thrown into Gehenna. Now if, as the Witnesses say, the man ceased to exist when his body was killed, what would be left afterwards to be thrown into Gehenna?

Likewise, in 2 Corinthians 5, the apostle Paul wrote of the body as "the earthly tent we live in," adding that he "would rather be away from the body and at home with the Lord," and warning that "we must all appear before the judgment seat of Christ, so that each one may receive good or evil, according to what he has done in the body" (vv. 1, 8–10, RSV). If the Jehovah's Witnesses were correct, what part of Paul could leave his body and go to be with the Lord?

You might also ask the JW to read Revelation 6:9–11 in his own Bible. There it speaks of "the souls of those slaughtered," asking God when their blood would be avenged. It adds that "a white robe was given to each of them; and they were told to rest a little while longer, until the number was filled also of their fellow slaves and their brothers who were about to be killed as they also had been." Yes, these souls had been killed, but they are depicted as being in God's presence and engaging in conversation with him.

See also the discussions of Psalm 146:3–4; Ecclesiastes 9:5; Luke 16:22–28; and Luke 23:43.

Psalm 37:9

Daniel 10:13, 21; 12:1

". . . . Michael, one of the foremost princes, came to help me. . . . Michael, the prince of you people. . . . And during that time

46

Michael will stand up, the great prince who is standing in behalf
of the sons of your people. . . ." (NWT)

The Watchtower Society teaches Jehovah's Witnesses
that Jesus Christ was a mere angel, who was born as a
human, died as a sacrifice for sins, and was raised up as
an angel once again. They refer to him as "Jesus Christ,
whom we understand from the Scriptures to be Michael
the archangel . . ." (*The Watchtower,* 2/15/79, p. 31). But
is that really what the Bible teaches? Or is it, rather, a
teaching that Watchtower leaders superimpose on
Scripture?

God's inspired Word mentions Michael five times—as
(1) "one of the foremost princes" (Dan. 10:13, NWT); (2)
"the prince of [Daniel's] people" (Dan. 10:21, NWT); (3) "the
great prince who is standing in behalf of the sons of [Dan-
iel's] people" (Dan. 12:1, NWT); (4) "the archangel" who
"had a difference with the Devil and was disputing about
Moses' body" but "did not dare to bring a judgment against
him in abusive terms" (Jude 9, NWT); and (5) a participant
in heavenly conflict when "Michael and his angels battled
with the dragon" (Rev. 12:7, NWT). Which of these verses
state that Michael is Jesus Christ? None of them! It is
necessary to read Scripture *plus* a complicated Watchtower argument to reach that conclusion.

The Society also turns for support to another verse that
does not use the name *Michael* but says that "the Lord
himself will descend from heaven with a commanding
call, with an archangel's voice and with God's trumpet"
(1 Thess. 4:16, NWT). But, if using an archangel's voice
makes the Lord an archangel, then having God's trumpet
makes him God—even though Watchtower leaders would
have us look at only the first part of the verse.

Does the Bible teach elsewhere that Jesus Christ is a
mere angel? To the contrary, the entire first chapter of
Hebrews was written to show the superiority of the Son

of God as compared to angels. Verse after verse contrasts
the angels with

> . . . His Son, whom He has appointed heir of all things,
> through whom also He made the worlds; who being the
> brightness of His glory and the express image of His per-
> son . . . having become so much better than the angels,
> as He has by inheritance obtained a more excellent name
> than they. For to which of the angels did He ever say:
> *"You are My Son, today I have begotten you"?* . . . But
> when He again brings the firstborn into the world, He
> says: *"Let all the angels of God worship Him."* And of the
> angels He says: *"Who makes His angels spirits and His
> ministers a flame of fire."* But to the Son He says: *"Your
> throne, O God, is forever and ever. . . ."* And: *"You,* LORD,
> *in the beginning laid the foundation of the earth. . . ."*
> (Heb. 1:2–8, 10, NKJV)

The Son is "the reflection" of the Father's glory "and the
exact representation of his very being, and he sustains all
things by the word of his power"—something no angel
could do—even according to the Watchtower's own translation of Hebrews 1:3 (NWT).

Moreover, good angels consistently refuse to accept worship. When the apostle John fell down to worship at the
feet of an angel, the angel rebuked him, saying, "Be careful! Do not do that! . . . Worship God" (Rev. 22:8–9, NWT).
But the Father's command concerning the Son is to "let
all God's angels worship him" (Heb. 1:6, NWT, 1961 edition). In later editions, the Watchtower Society changed
"worship" to "obeisance" at Hebrew 1:6. Still, regardless
of how it is translated, the same Greek word *proskuneo*
is used at both Rev. 22:8–9 and Hebrews 1:6. The *proskuneo* (worship or obeisance) that angels refuse to accept,
but say to give only to God, is the same *proskuneo* (worship or obeisance) that the Father commands to be given
to the Son at Hebrews 1:6. So, the Son cannot be an angel,
but must be God. (See discussion of Heb. 1:6.)

Persons who stop following the Watchtower organization, and start following Jesus Christ, soon come to appreciate that he is no mere angel. This realization is important, in order that they may "honor the Son just as they honor the Father" (John 5:23, NWT).

See also the discussions of Isaiah 9:6; John 1:1; John 20:28; Colossians 1:15; Revelation 1:7–8; and Revelation 3:14.

4

Verse-by-Verse Answers for JW's—New Testament

Matthew

Matthew 3:11

[John the Baptist said:] "He will baptize you with the Holy Spirit and fire." (NKJV)

According to the Watchtower Society's 1982 book *You Can Live Forever in Paradise on Earth* (p. 40), "John the Baptizer said that Jesus would baptize with holy spirit, even as John had been baptizing with water. Hence, in the same way that water is not a person, holy spirit is not a person. (Matthew 3:11)"

How valid is this Jehovah's Witness reasoning against the personality of the Holy Spirit? Not valid at all!—because the same "baptism argument" could be used against the personality of Jesus Christ, who obviously walked the earth as a person. For example, Romans 6:3 says: "Do you not know that all of us who have been *baptized into Christ Jesus* were baptized into his death?" (RSV, italics added). "Hence, in the same way that death is not a person, Jesus Christ is not a person," the parallel argument would run. And Galatians 3:27 says, that "all of you who were baptized into Christ have been clothed with Christ" (NIV).

Matthew 3:11

Here the line of thought would be: "Since people can be baptized into Christ and clothed with Christ, he must not be a person." Do these comparisons disprove the personality of Christ? No! Then, neither does the "baptism argument" disprove the personality of the Holy Spirit.

See the discussion of the "pouring out" and "filling" with the Holy Spirit, under Acts 2:4. For further proof of the personality and deity of the Holy Spirit, see also John 16:13; Acts 5:3–4; Romans 8:26–27; and 1 Corinthians 6:19.

Matthew 6:9

"You must pray, then, this way: 'Our Father in the heavens, let your name be sanctified.' " (NWT)

Jehovah's Witnesses point out that God's name must be sanctified, and thus they "prove" that we must use the name *Jehovah,* in order for our prayers to be heard by God. But is that what Jesus taught? Did he begin his own prayers with the expression "Jehovah God," as the Witnesses do?

Not at all! While expressing concern in the prayer that God's name be sanctified or hallowed (treated as sacred or holy), Jesus taught his disciples to pray to "our Father," not to "Jehovah God." He said, "You must pray, then, this way: 'Our Father. . . .' "

Many of Jesus' own personal prayers are also recorded in the Bible, and in these he sets the same example:

"Father, I thank you . . ." (John 11:41, NWT).

"*Abba,* Father, all things are possible to you . . ." (Mark 14:36, NWT).

"Father, the hour has come . . ." (John 17:1, NWT).

Witnesses might object by saying, "Jesus had a close, special relationship with the Father. That's why he did not address him as 'Jehovah.' " We might acknowledge that there is some truth to that, but Jesus' purpose was to bring all of his disciples into a close, special relationship with

God, too. "No one comes to the Father except through me," Jesus taught (John 14:6, NWT). Of Christians who come to the Father through Jesus, the Bible says: ". . . you have received the Spirit of adoption by whom we cry out, 'Abba, Father.' The Spirit Himself bears witness with our spirit that we are children of God" (Rom. 8:15–16, NKJV).

It is obvious that Jesus' words at Matthew 6:9 definitely do *not* teach a need to use the name *Jehovah* in prayer.

Matthew 14:6–10

> But when Herod's birthday came. . . . he sent and had John beheaded in the prison. (RSV)

This verse is cited frequently by Jehovah's Witnesses in connection with their organization's prohibition against birthday celebrations. See the discussion of Genesis 40:20–22.

Matthew 24:3

> Now as He sat on the Mount of Olives, the disciples came to Him privately, saying, "Tell us, when will these things be? And what will be the sign of Your coming, and of the end of the age?" And Jesus answered and said to them: "Take heed that no one deceives you." (NKJV)

Unfortunately, someone has already deceived Jehovah's Witnesses, and we must take care that they do not deceive us. The Watchtower Society substitutes "presence" for "coming" in their translation, using this as a basis for teaching followers that Jesus returned invisibly in the year 1914 and has been present ever since. Doing what? Why, directing the Watchtower organization, naturally!

In the same context, Jesus warned against just such a deception: "Then many false prophets will rise up and deceive many. . . . Then if anyone says to you, 'Look, here is the Christ!' or 'There!' do not believe it. For false christs and false prophets will arise and show great signs and wonders, so as to deceive, if possible, even the elect. See, I have told you beforehand. Therefore if they say to you, 'Look, He is in the desert!' do not go out; or 'Look, He is in the inner rooms!' do not believe it" (vv. 11, 23–26, NKJV).

In effect, the Watchtower leaders claim that Christ is "in the inner rooms" of their organization. You must come to them, in order to receive instructions from him. Happily, though, there is an abundance of evidence to help an individual Jehovah's Witness to see through this deception.

First of all, there is the matter of prophecy. The Watchtower Society has such a long history of failed prophecies that it qualifies for the label "false prophet" many times over. (See our discussion of Deut. 18:20–22 for specific examples of what the organization prophesied for the years 1914, 1925, and 1975.)

There is also the fact that their story keeps changing. It is one thing to claim that Christ returned invisibly in 1914, but another thing to make that claim after you have already spent fifty years telling people that he returned invisibly in 1874—and then changed your mind. Yet the JW organization has done just that. When *The Watchtower* magazine began publication back in 1879, it was originally titled *Zion's Watch Tower and Herald of Christ's Presence*. And, fifty years later, in the book *Prophecy* by J. F. Rutherford, this 1874 "presence" was still being heralded: "The Scriptural proof is that the second presence of the Lord Jesus Christ began in 1874 A.D." (p. 65). Now the Society says that he returned in 1914. So, by their own admission, they were false heralds, announcing the presence of a Christ who was not there, from 1874 until 1914.

Claiming that Christ is invisibly present and ruling on earth through them, the JW leaders tell their followers, "In the first century, Jerusalem was the place from which direction was given the Christian organization (Acts 15:1, 2). But today such direction is provided from Brooklyn, New York" (*The Watchtower,* 12/1/82, p. 23). In view of the evidence, though, should an individual Jehovah's Witness continue in fearful obedience to these men? Let Scripture answer: "If a prophet speaks in the name of the LORD and what he says does not come true, then it is not the LORD's message. That prophet has spoken on his own authority, and you are not to fear him" (Deut. 18:22, TEV).

See also the discussions of Exodus 3:15; Deuteronomy 18:20–22; Isaiah 43:10; Matthew 24:14; and Matthew 24:45.

Matthew 24:14

"And this good news of the kingdom will be preached in all the inhabited earth for a witness to all the nations; and then the end will come." (NWT)

This verse is one of Jehovah's Witnesses' all-time favorites. But they read into it a number of thoughts that go beyond what it says. They believe that Jesus Christ returned invisibly in the year A.D. 1914 and "established" God's kingdom in heaven at that time, with the Watchtower Society as his visible agency on earth. So, in order to receive everlasting life, people need to "come to Jehovah's organization for salvation" (*The Watchtower,* 11/15/81, p. 21).

When Jehovah's Witnesses preach their "gospel" or "good news" of the kingdom, they are actually preaching the doctrine of Christ's invisible return in 1914. They freely acknowledge that the "good news" they preach is not the same as the gospel or Good News preached by Christians down through the centuries. But they think it is wonderful that they have a *different* good news:

... the Kingdom witnessing of Jehovah's Witnesses since 1914 has been something far different from what Christendom's missionaries have published both before and since 1914. "Different"—how so? ... What Jehovah's

55

Witnesses have preached world wide since 1918 is something unique . . . the preaching of this good news of the Messianic kingdom as having been established in the heavens in 1914. . . . (*The Watchtower,* 10/1/80, pp. 28–29)

But the Bible plainly warns against the preaching of another gospel:

However, even if we or an angel out of heaven were to declare to you as good news something beyond what we declared to you as good news, let him be accursed. As we have said above, I also now say again, Whoever it is that is declaring to you as good news something beyond what you accepted, let him be accursed. (Gal. 1:8–9, NWT)

Ask the Jehovah's Witness, "Did the apostle Paul teach the disciples in Galatia that Christ would return in 1914 and set up a visible organization with headquarters in Brooklyn, New York?" If not, then the Watchtower leaders' "good news" is "something beyond" what the Galatians accepted—placing them under God's curse for teaching another gospel.

See also the discussions of Deuteronomy 18:20–22; Matthew 24:3; and Matthew 24:34.

Matthew 24:34

"Assuredly, I say to you, this generation will by no means pass away till all these things are fulfilled." (NKJV)

Which generation? The subject is a matter of debate among Christian Bible readers—but not among Jehovah's Witnesses, because their organization has told them specifically that "the evidence points to the 1914 generation as the generation spoken of by Jesus. Thus, 'this generation will by no means pass away until all these things (including the apocalypse) occur' " (*The Watchtower,* 2/15/86, p. 5).

For many years, each issue of their *Awake!* magazine

has featured this statement of purpose on page 2: "Most importantly, this magazine builds confidence in the Creator's promise of a peaceful and secure New Order before the generation that saw the events of 1914 passes away." The *Awake!* issue of October 8, 1968, defined the generation even more precisely by saying, "Jesus was obviously speaking about those who were old enough to witness *with understanding* what took place," suggesting that these would be "youngsters 15 years of age" (p. 13, italics theirs). They said most definitely that "the 'generation' logically would not apply to babies born during World War I" (*The Watchtower,* 10/1/78, p. 31).

One need only calculate that someone fifteen years old in 1914 would be twenty-five years old in 1924, thirty-five years old in 1934—and eighty-five years old in 1984—to realize that the Watchtower's "generation that will not pass away" was almost gone by the mid-1980s. The prophecy was about to fail. But, rather than change the prophecy, JW leaders simply stretched the generation. Instead of fifteen-year-olds, who could witness "with understanding" what took place in 1914, they began to indicate instead that the generation would be made up of "those born around the time" (the very babies that they had earlier excluded!), saying: "If Jesus used 'generation' in that sense and we apply it to 1914, then the babies of that generation are now 70 years old or older" (*The Watchtower,* 5/15/84, p. 5).

Genuine Christians pray eagerly for the Lord to come again. And we wait and watch for his coming. But persons who make false prophecies fall into the categories of those the Lord warned us to watch out for: "For false christs and false prophets will arise and show great signs and wonders, so as to deceive, if possible, even the elect" (Matt. 24:24, NKJV).

For information on the Watchtower organization's hundred-year history of false prophesying, see our discussion of Deuteronomy 18:20–22.

Matthew 24:45-47

"Who really is the faithful and discreet slave whom his master appointed over his domestics, to give them their food at the proper time? Happy is that slave if his master on arriving finds him doing so. Truly I say to you, He will appoint him over all his belongings." (NWT)

This is a key text for Jehovah's Witnesses. They attach a unique interpretation to the parable. Instead of seeing it as an exhortation to each Christian to be a faithful and diligent "slave" for Christ, they believe that their organization represents *the* faithful and discreet slave, divinely appointed to dispense "spiritual food" to the household of faith. This interpretation gives Watchtower headquarters tremendous power and authority in the eyes of the average Witness.

For example, note how *The Watchtower* of December 1, 1981, elevates the organization above the Bible and makes gaining everlasting life contingent on following the Watchtower Society:

Jehovah God has also provided his visible organization, his "faithful and discreet slave," made up of spirit-anointed ones, to help Christians in all nations to understand and apply properly the Bible in their lives. Unless we are in touch with this channel of communication that God is using, we will not progress along the road to life, no matter how much Bible reading we do [p. 27].

Favored indeed are all those who serve loyally with the "faithful and discreet slave" organization, Jehovah's visible agent of communication! Theirs is the wise choice, for their pathway leads on to the precious goal of everlasting life . . . [p. 31].

Perhaps I should mention here, as a personal aside, that the above statements, especially the one on page 27, which elevates the organization above the Bible, became "the last straw"—the straw that broke the camel's back—in my relationship with the Watchtower Society. It was after reading this that I began speaking out, questioning the organization's claims publicly at Kingdom Hall meetings and secretly publishing my newsletter, *Comments from the Friends*, the first issue of which dealt with the above quote. (See chapter seven, "The Author's Testimony," for further details.) Unfortunately, the vast majority of Jehovah's Witnesses remain conditioned to the extent that they applaud such statements and blindly follow the Society wherever it leads.

Originally, it was Charles Taze Russell, the founder and first president of the Watchtower Society, who was viewed personally and individually as the "faithful and wise servant" of Matthew 24:45. After his death, there occurred a major split in the organization, with supporters of the new president, Joseph F. Rutherford, seizing complete control, and members loyal to Pastor Russell leaving to form other sects, some of which continue to exist today. These modern-day Russellite groups continue to print the pastor's books and to view him as God's special messenger to the church. "Judge" Rutherford's followers insisted that Russell never claimed to be the "faithful and wise servant," but that the Watchtower corporation as a whole was God's chosen instrument.

It is very difficult to disabuse Jehovah's Witnesses of this belief. They accept whatever the Society tells them *because* the Society is God's channel of communication, which, in turn, they believe *because* it is the only religious organization on earth teaching the truth—a conclusion they defend *because* they accept everything the Society tells them. Although this is circular reasoning, it is the way that Jehovah's Witnesses think. At some point after the so-called Bible study, or indoctrination program, that originally brings an individual into the organization, his or her chain of reasoning is twisted about and connected together end-to-end, so that the JW thinks in circles instead of in a straight line. That's why you can go 'round and 'round with a Witness and get nowhere. It could be called *brainwashing*.

The key to breaking that vicious circle is to give the individual some information that will jar his thinking enough to get his mind off the well-worn track that it has learned to function in. This can be a long, slow process. Much prayer and persistence is required. But it can be done.

For help, see chapter six on techniques for sharing the gospel.

Matthew 26:27

> And he took a cup, and when he had given thanks he gave it to them, saying, "Drink of it, all of you." (RSV)

The Watchtower Society has taught its followers not to obey these clear instructions from Jesus Christ. When Jehovah's Witnesses hold their annual communion celebration, the loaf and the cup are passed from hand to hand with hardly anyone partaking. (Statistics reported in the January 1, 1986, *Watchtower* magazine revealed that, of 7,792,109 in attendance at the celebration in 1985, only 9,051 partook. So, most of the 49,716 worldwide congregations of Jehovah's Witnesses had no partakers at all in their midst.)

In failing to "drink of it, all of you" as Jesus commanded, the Witnesses are responding instead to instructions from their leaders, who have taught them that new believers since the year 1935 cannot share in the New Covenant mediated by Jesus Christ (Heb. 12:24); "Those of the 'other sheep' class are not in the new covenant and so do not partake" (*The Watchtower*, 2/15/86, p. 15).

But, speaking of the lifesaving covenant represented in the communion loaf and cup, Jesus said, "Unless you eat the flesh of the Son of man and drink his blood, you have no life in yourselves" (John 6:53, NWT). If Witnesses exclude themselves from the New Covenant, they exclude themselves from eternal life.

Ask a Jehovah's Witness to show you a Bible verse where Jesus set the year 1935 as an expiration date for his instructions regarding communion. There is no such verse. Rather, he said, "Keep doing this in remembrance of me" (Luke 22:19, NWT).

See also the discussion at Revelation 7:9 for more information on the "1935 doctrine," and John 10:16 regarding the "other sheep."

Mark

Mark 1:8

"I have baptized you with water; but he will baptize you with the Holy Spirit." (RSV)

See discussion of the same quote at Matthew 3:11.

Mark 6:21–25

. . . Herod on his birthday gave a banquet. . . . And she came in immediately with haste to the king, and asked, saying, "I want you to give me at once the head of John the Baptist on a platter." (RSV)

This is one of the three passages that Jehovah's Witnesses use to argue against celebrating birthdays. See our discussion of Genesis 40:20–22.

Mark 12:29

And Jesus answered him, The first of all the commandments is, Hear, O Israel; The Lord our God is one Lord. (KJV)

This is a text that Jehovah's Witnesses cite in presenting their case against the doctrine of the Trinity. They focus on the statement that God is *one*. But what they fail to understand is that the New Testament reveals this as a composite oneness.

There is a good reason why the pre-Christian Jews did not grasp the composite oneness of God: it had not yet been revealed. But, in the case of Jehovah's Witnesses, the revealed truth of Scripture has been hidden from their eyes by their leaders.

Let the Witness know that you agree with him that God is one God. Tell the JW that you do not believe in three Gods. Then ask a few questions to stimulate the JW's reasoning on the matter: Can the one True God listen to different people praying at the same time? Could he speak to more than one person at the same time, if he chose to do so? Can he do things in more than one place at the same time?

Tell the Witness that you would like him to consider a hypothetical question: "Suppose God decided to personally visit the earth? Would he have to leave heaven in order to do so? Or could he visit the earth, while still remaining in heaven to run the universe?" (The Witness will not want to answer.) Go on to say: "I'm not asking you to agree that God *did* do such a thing. But do you think that he *could* do that, if he wanted to?" Without attempting an accurate description or definition of the Trinity, help the Witness to open his mind to the possibility that God's oneness might be composite.

Then proceed to look up and read these passages with the JW: Genesis 18:1–2; 1 Corinthians 6:19; Colossians 2:9; and Revelation 1:7–8. (See discussions of these verses.)

Luke

Luke 3:16

John answered them all, "I baptize you with water . . . he will baptize you with the Holy Spirit and with fire." (RSV)

See discussion of the same quote at Matthew 3:11.

Luke 16:22 –24, 27 –28

> Now in course of time the beggar died and he was carried off by the angels to the bosom [position] of Abraham. Also, the rich man died and was buried. And in Hades he lifted up his eyes, he existing in torments, and he saw Abraham afar off and Lazarus in the bosom [position] with him. So he called and said, "Father Abraham, have mercy on me and send Lazarus to dip the tip of his finger in water and cool my tongue, because I am in anguish in this blazing fire. . . . send him to the house of my father, for I have five brothers, in order that he may give them a thorough witness, that they also should not get into this place of torment." (NWT)

Jehovah's Witnesses believe their organization's teaching that *hades* is simply the grave and that there is no conscious existence for the dead until a future resurrection. But, since Jesus' words in the verses above *do* speak of such conscious existence, the Watchtower Society has to do something to negate those words. So they point out that the account is a parable, or illustration, and apply a purely symbolic meaning to everything in the story.

In the Watchtower's interpretation, Lazarus pictures Jesus' disciples, the rich man pictures the Jewish religious leaders, Abraham pictures Jehovah God, the death of each pictures a change of conditions for each group while here on earth, and the torments of the rich man picture the public exposure of Jewish religious leaders by the Apostles' preaching. Therefore, Jesus was not really talking about the condition of the dead in Luke 16, according to the Watchtower Society.

Christians, too, will generally agree that the story of the rich man and Lazarus is one of Jesus' many parables. But an examination of the Lord's other parables reveals that all of them were illustrations based on real-life situations. For example, a prodigal son returned home after squandering his money; a man found a buried treasure in a field, hid it again, and sold everything he had in order to buy that field; a king put on a wedding feast for his son; a slaveowner traveled abroad and then returned home to his slaves; a man constructed a vineyard, leased it out to others, but had difficulty collecting what they owed him; and so on.

Young men really did leave home and squander their inheritance, and Jesus used his audience's familiarity with such circumstances to illustrate things relating to the kingdom. People really did find buried treasure, put on wedding feasts, leave slaves in charge while traveling abroad, lease vineyards, and so on, and Jesus used his listeners' familiarity with these situations to illustrate spiritual things. So, if the story of the rich man and Lazarus is like all the rest of Jesus' parables, it also must use a real situation to illustrate spiritual things. People must really have a conscious existence after death, and some of them must really be "in torments," deeply regretting their past life. Regardless of what the parable illustrates, the basic story, like the other stories Jesus told, must be taken from real life.

Remembering what the Bible reveals to us about Jesus' mercy and compassion and love, we know that God is not a cruel, unfeeling monster who delights in tormenting people. If we truly know him, we realize that he is more kind and loving than we are. So, if we are unable to reconcile God's goodness with Jesus' teaching on the condition of the dead, the problem must lie with us, in our limited comprehension, rather than with God. Abraham faced a similar problem when he learned that God was about to rain fire and brimstone on Sodom and Gomorrah. He questioned God, even asking, "Shall not the Judge of all the earth do right?" (Gen. 18:25). Therefore, a person who is upset by Jesus' teaching should follow Abraham's example by taking the matter to God in prayer and asking for help to trust in him fully, even in matters that are beyond human understanding.

But the solution is not to be found in denying what the Bible plainly says. Although Jesus Christ was by far the most loving and compassionate person ever to walk the earth, he also had the most to say about the unpleasantness facing people after death. He said, for example:

"The Son of man will send his angels, and they will gather out of his kingdom all causes of sin and all evildoers, and throw them into the furnace of fire; there men will weep and gnash their teeth." (Matt. 13:41–42, RSV)

"But he will say, 'I tell you, I do not know where you come from; depart from me, all you workers of iniquity!' There you will weep and gnash your teeth, when you see Abraham and Isaac and Jacob and all the prophets in the kingdom of God and you yourselves thrust out." (Luke 13:27–28, RSV)

"So it will be at the end of the age. The angels will come out and separate the evil from the righteous, and throw them into the furnace of fire; there men will weep and gnash their teeth." (Matt. 13:49–50, RSV)

"Then the king said to the attendants, 'Bind him hand and foot, and cast him into the outer darkness; there men will weep and gnash their teeth.' " (Matt. 22:13, RSV)

"The master of that servant will come on a day when he does not expect him and at an hour he is not aware of. He will cut him to pieces and assign him a place with the hypocrites, where there will be weeping and gnashing of teeth." (Matt. 24:50–51, NIV)

"The master of that servant will come on a day when he does not expect him and at an hour he is not aware of. He will cut him to pieces and assign him a place with the unbelievers. That servant who knows his master's will and does not get ready or does not do what his master wants will be beaten with many blows. But the one who does not know and does things deserving punishment will be beaten with few blows. . . ." (Luke 12:46–48, NIV)

65

" 'And throw the good-for-nothing slave out into the darkness outside. There is where his weeping and the gnashing of his teeth will be.' " (Matt. 25:30, NWT)

". . . but woe to that man by whom the Son of man is betrayed! It would have been better for that man if he had not been born." [Author's note: If he had not been born, the betrayer would have been nonexistent. But nonexistence was *better* than the punishment now in store for him. So, the Watchtower must be wrong in its teaching that Judas' death plunged him into eternal nonexistence.] (Matt. 26:24, RSV)

". . . it is finer for you to enter one-eyed into the kingdom of God than with two eyes to be pitched into Gehenna, where their maggot does not die and the fire is not put out." (Mark 9:47–48, NWT)

"Rejoice in that day and leap, for, look! your reward is great in heaven. . . . But woe to you rich persons, because you are having your consolation in full. Woe to you who are filled up now, because you will go hungry. Woe, you who are laughing now, because you will mourn and weep." (Luke 6:23–25, NWT)

"Moreover, I say to you, my friends, Do not fear those who kill the body and after this are not able to do anything more. But I will indicate to you whom to fear: Fear him who after killing has authority to throw into Gehenna. Yes, I tell you, fear this One." (Luke 12:4–5, NWT)

And in the revelation that Jesus gave to the aged apostle John, the Lord's angelic messenger says,

"If anyone worships the wild beast and its image, and receives a mark on his forehead or upon his hand, he will also drink of the wine of the anger of God that is poured out undiluted into the cup of his wrath, and he shall be tormented with fire and sulphur in the sight of the holy

angels and in the sight of the Lamb. And the smoke of
their torment ascends forever and ever, and day and night
they have no rest. .... (Rev. 14:9–11, NWT)

Conclude by asking the Jehovah's Witness, "If someone
never read any Watchtower Society publications, but only
read Jesus' words, what would he believe on this subject?
What did Bible readers believe for centuries before Watchtower founder 'Pastor' Russell came along in the late 1800s
and taught his no-hell doctrine?"

The Lord used figurative language—darkness, fire, torment, exclusion—but the point is clear: Jesus taught that
disobedient mankind faces some sort of unpleasantness
after death, and that he came as Savior to rescue us from
such a fate.

Luke 22:19

Also, he took a loaf, gave thanks, broke it, and gave it to
them, saying: "This means my body which is to be given in your
behalf. Keep doing this in remembrance of me." (NWT)

The Watchtower organization teaches that new converts
since the year 1935 do not become part of the Christian
congregation, the body of Christ, and therefore that such
individuals "do not partake of the emblems" at communion (*The Truth that Leads to Eternal Life,* Watchtower
Society, 1968, p. 80). So, even though their own Bible says
to "keep doing this," the vast majority of Jehovah's Witnesses do not.

For further details, see the discussions at Matthew 26:27
and Revelation 7:9.

Luke 23:43

And he said to him, "Truly, I say to you, today you will be with
me in Paradise." (RSV)

Compare the above with how the same verse is rendered in the Jehovah's Witnesses' *New World Translation*: "And he said to him: 'Truly I tell you today, You will be with me in Paradise.' "

Do you notice the difference? It is a very small change, but very significant. The Watchtower Society's translators have moved the comma from *before* the word "today" to *after* it. This moves the adverb "today" from the second half of the sentence to the first half. So, instead of "today" identifying the time when the repentant evildoer on the cross will be with the Lord "in Paradise," the text is changed so that "today" appears to identify simply the time when Jesus was speaking.

This is another case in which JW leaders have changed the Bible to fit their doctrines. They teach that the man who turned to the Lord on the cross and said, "Jesus, remember me when you come into your kingdom" (v. 42), did *not* go to be with Christ in Paradise that day. Rather, they claim that he was annihilated at death, has not existed anywhere at all for the past two thousand years, and will eventually get to be with the Lord in Paradise at some time during the future millennium. It was difficult for Jehovah's Witnesses to teach this doctrine in view of Jesus' words to the dying man. Therefore, when they produced their own Bible, they changed his words—or at least the punctuation, which changes the meaning of the words.

If you challenge Witnesses on this point, they will likely defend the change by reading from the footnote to verse 43 in the 1984 reference edition of their *New World Translation:* "Although WH [the Westcott and Hort Greek text] puts a comma in the Gr. text before the word for 'today,' commas were not used in Gr. uncial mss. In keeping with the context, we omit the comma before 'today.' " However, what the JW translators should really say is that "in keeping with their *doctrine*," they move the comma.

However, since they mention context, it would be useful to look at the rest of the Book of Luke and the other three

Gospels. Jesus used the expression "truly I tell you," or "truly I say to you," on many different occasions. (The same Greek word is rendered both "tell" and "say.") How did the New World Bible Translation Committee punctuate the same expression in every other place where it appears? Where did all the commas go?

There is a very easy way to find out. Ask the Jehovah's Witness you are speaking with to show you the *Comprehensive Concordance* that the Watchtower Society published in 1973 for the *New World Translation*. Since the concordance is arranged alphabetically, have the Witness look up the word "truly." There you will find a convenient listing of the six verses where the Lord used this same expression in the Gospel of Luke, as well as all seventy-one passages where he used it in the four Gospels. In addition to the chapter-and-verse numbers, the concordance shows the words immediately before and after "truly" in each text. Just glance at the list: the commas all line up, *except* for Luke 23:43. This is the only verse that they punctuated differently, so as to include the time element in the first half of the sentence—obvious proof that Watchtower translators altered this verse to fit the sect's doctrines.

For further discussion on what happens to people when they die, see Psalm 146:3-4 and Luke 16:22-28.

For additional examples of distortions in the *New World Translation,* see our chapter two, "The Bible That Jehovah's Witnesses Use," as well as the discussions of Romans 14:7-9 and Hebrews 1:6.

Luke 24:36-39

While they were speaking of these things he himself stood in their midst. . . . But because they were terrified, and had become frightened, they were imagining they beheld a spirit. So he said to them: "Why are you troubled, and why is it doubts come up in your hearts? See my hands and my feet, that it is I

myself; feel me and see, because a spirit does not have flesh
and bones just as you behold that I have." (NWT)

In contrast to the above words in their own Bible, Jehovah's Witness leaders teach that the resurrected Christ
is a spirit and that: "The human body of flesh, which Jesus
Christ laid down forever as a ransom sacrifice, was disposed of by God's power, but not by fire on the altar of the
temple in Jerusalem. The flesh of a sacrifice is always
disposed of and put out of existence, so not corrupting"
(Watchtower book *Things in Which It Is Impossible for
God to Lie,* 1965, p. 354). They also say: "Following his
resurrection, Jesus did not always appear in the same
body of flesh [perhaps to reinforce in their minds the fact
that he was then a spirit]" (Watchtower book *Reasoning
from the Scriptures,* 1985, p. 335).

Obviously, the Jehovah's Witness organization would
have us believe the opposite of what Scripture teaches on
this point. They insist that Christ's body was not resurrected but disposed of, and that he became a spirit. If that
were true, then his statements at Luke 24:36–39 would
have been lies; and his showing the disciples the nail scars
in his hands and feet, and inviting them to feel his flesh
and bones, would have been a clever trick to deceive them.

Besides discussing the above, you might also ask Jehovah's Witnesses to read the verses where Jesus had originally foretold what would happen to his body: "In answer
Jesus said to them: 'Break down this temple, and in three
days I will raise it up.' Therefore the Jews said: 'This temple was built in forty-six years, and will you raise it up in
three days?' But he was talking about the temple of his
body" (John 2:19–21, NWT).

The Witnesses have a choice to make—to believe what
Jesus said about his bodily resurrection, or to believe what
the Watchtower says.

John

John 1:1

In the beginning was the Word, and the Word was with God, and the Word was God. (ASV)

Until around 1950, Jehovah's Witnesses carried with them a copy of the American Standard Version of the Bible (because it features the name *Jehovah* throughout the Old Testament). But they faced the embarrassing problem of trying to deny the deity of Christ, while the very Bible they held in their hand said plainly that "the Word was God." This problem was solved when the Watchtower Society published its own *New World Translation of the Holy Scriptures.*

Now, when Christians refer JWs to John 1:1, the Witnesses can answer, "That's not in *my* Bible!" They can turn to John 1:1 in their own translation, and read ". . . the Word was a god."

By reducing Jesus Christ to "a god," the Watchtower places him among the "many 'gods' and many 'lords' " of 1 Corinthians 8:5—on the same level as Satan, "the god of this system of things" (2 Cor. 4:4, NWT).

The Watchtower Society presents the *New World Translation* as the anonymous work of the New World Bible Translation Committee—and resists all efforts to identify the members of the committee. They say they do this in order that all *credit* for the work will go to God. But an unbiased observer will quickly note that such anonymity also shields the translators from any *blame* for errors or distortions in their renderings. And it prevents scholars from checking their credentials. In fact, defectors who have quit Watchtower headquarters in recent years have identified the alleged members of the committee, revealing that none of them was expert in Hebrew, Greek, or Ara-

71

maic—the original languages from which the Bible must be translated.

For many years Jehovah's Witnesses turned for support of their "a god" rendering to *The New Testament* (1937) by Johannes Greber, since Greber also translated it as ". . . the Word was a god." Watchtower Society publications quote or cite Greber in support of this and other renderings, as follows:

Aid to Bible Understanding (1969), pages 1134 and 1669

"Make Sure of All Things—Hold Fast to What Is Fine" (1965), page 489

The Watchtower, 9/15/62, page 554

The Watchtower, 10/15/75, page 640

The Watchtower, 4/15/76, page 231

"The Word"—Who Is He? According to John (1962), page 5

However, after ex-Witnesses gave considerable publicity to the fact that Greber was a spiritist who claimed that spirits showed him what words to use in his translation, *The Watchtower* (4/1/83) said on page 31:

> This translation was used occasionally in support of renderings of Matthew 27:52, 53 and John 1:1, as given in the *New World Translation* and other authoritative Bible versions. But as indicated in a foreword to the 1980 edition of *The New Testament* by Johannes Greber, this translator relied on "God's Spirit World" to clarify for him how he should translate difficult passages. It is stated: "His wife, a medium of God's Spirit world was often instrumental in conveying the correct answers from God's Messengers to Pastor Greber." *The Watchtower* has deemed it improper to make use of a translation that has such a close rapport with spiritism. (Deuteronomy 18:10–12) The scholarship that forms the basis for the rendering of the

above-cited texts in the *New World Translation* is sound
and for this reason does not depend at all on Greber's
translation for authority. Nothing is lost, therefore, by
ceasing to use his *New Testament.*

Thus, it appeared that the Society had only just then
discovered Greber's spiritistic connections and immediately repented of using him for support. However, this,
too, was yet another deception—because the JW organization already knew of Greber's spiritism back in 1956.
The Watchtower of February 15, 1956, contains nearly a
full page devoted to warning readers *against* Johannes
Greber and his translation. It refers to his book titled
*Communication with the Spirit-World: Its Laws and Its
Purpose* and states, "Very plainly the spirits in which ex-
priest Greber believes helped him in his translation" (*The
Watchtower,* 2/15/56, p. 111).

Aside from Greber's *New Testament* and the Watch-
tower Society's slanted version, other English-language
Bible translations are nearly unanimous in rendering John
1:1 as ". . . the Word was God." And this is consistent with
the declaration by the apostle Thomas, also found in John's
Gospel, calling Jesus "My Lord and my God!" (John 20:28).
The JW *New World Translation* still calls Jesus "God" in
John 20:28 and Isaiah 9:6. In fact, their 1985 *Kingdom
Interlinear* version reveals that the Greek literally says
Jesus is "the God" (HO THEOS) in John 20:28.

Anyone who believes that the Father is God, while the
Son is "a god" should read Isaiah 43 and 44, where the
inspired Word dismisses such a notion: "Before Me no God
was formed, nor shall there be after Me. I, even I, am the
LORD, and beside Me there is no savior. . . . is there *a
god* beside me? There is no other Rock; I know of none!"
(Isa. 43:10–11; 44:8, MLB italics added).

For additional information on the deity of Christ and
attempts by Watchtower translators to hide it in their
Bible, see the discussions of Genesis 18:1–2; Exodus 3:14;

Psalm 110:1; Isaiah 9:6; Daniel 10:13, 21; John 8:57–58; John 20:28; and Hebrews 1:6.

John 3:3, 7

> In answer Jesus said to him: "Most truly I say to you, Unless anyone is born again, he cannot see the kingdom of God. . . . You people must be born again." (NWT)

Even though these words appear in their own Bible, Jehovah's Witnesses do not believe that they must be born again. "That doesn't apply to me. It's only for the hundred and forty-four thousand anointed ones. I belong to the 'great crowd' who will live on the earth under Kingdom rule" is the typical answer a JW will give when asked if he has been born again. (See the discussions of John 10:16 and Revelation 7:4 and 7:9, for information about their beliefs on the 144,000 and the "great crowd" of "other sheep.") The organization has specifically taught them: "The 'other sheep' do not need any such rebirth, for their goal is life everlasting in the restored earthly paradise as subjects of the Kingdom" (*The Watchtower*, 2/15/86, p. 14).

The first step to take is to ask the Witness to read with you in the Watchtower's own translation what the Bible actually says about being born again at John 3:3–15. Emphasize that Jesus did not allow for exceptions when he said, "Unless *anyone* is born again, he cannot see the kingdom of God" (v. 3).

Then turn to 1 John 5:1, where the *New World Translation* says, "Everyone believing that Jesus is the Christ has been born from God. . . ." Ask the JW whether the expression "everyone believing" leaves anyone out.

Next have the Witness go to Galatians 4:5–6, where the Bible explains that Christ came in order "that we, in turn, might receive the adoption as sons. Now because you are sons, God has sent forth the spirit of his Son into our hearts and it cries out: 'Abba, Father!' " (NWT). Ask him if he has been adopted as a child of God by personally receiving the Spirit of the Son of God, Jesus Christ, into his heart, as described there. In harmony with Watchtower doctrine, he will answer, "No!"

Finally, turn to Romans 8. First direct the JW to verses 14 through 16, showing him that the chapter is discussing the same subject: receiving the "spirit of adoption" and crying out "*Abba,* Father!"—which the Witness says does not apply to him. And then go back to the beginning of Romans 8 and read with him verses 1 through 7, commenting on the contrast between walking in the flesh and walking "in the spirit." Now you are ready to drive home the crucial point of verses 8 and 9:

> So those who are in harmony with the flesh *cannot please God.* However, you are in harmony, not with the flesh, but with the spirit, *if* God's spirit truly dwells in you. But *if* anyone *does not have Christ's spirit,* this one does not belong to him. (NWT, italics added)

Remind the Witness that he has admitted that he has not received Christ's Spirit to dwell in his heart by being born again through adoption as a child of God. In the light of verses 8 and 9, therefore, can he reach any conclusion other than that *he cannot please God, and he does not belong to Christ?*

At this point, you will probably have to re-read Romans 8 with him. Since the passage is one seldom covered in Kingdom Hall Bible-study classes, the average Jehovah's Witness is unaware of what it says. But, when a Witness finally grasps its meaning, it can have a devastating effect. I know that firsthand—because, when I finally encountered those verses after thirteen years in the Watchtower organization, they nearly knocked me off my feet. Within a short time I was confessing my need of the Savior and praying to receive Christ's Spirit into my heart. And—Praise God!—he answered my prayer.

John 3:3, 7

But don't be disappointed if the Jehovah's Witness you are talking to responds with an argument instead of a prayer. In my own case, I read Romans 8 at a time when several weeks of soul-searching and intense Bible reading had already led me to leave the organization. It usually takes a considerable period of time—perhaps even months or years—for the needed information to sink in and produce change in a JW. Plant carefully and water patiently—then God will make it grow! (1 Cor. 3:6).

John 4:23

"Nevertheless, the hour is coming, and it is now, when the true worshipers will worship the Father with spirit and truth, for indeed, the Father is looking for suchlike ones to worship him." (NWT)

Jehovah's Witnesses often use this verse in their house-to-house preaching work. After greeting the householder, they ask, "Whom do you worship as God? What is his name?" If the answer given is "the Lord," or "God," the JW will respond, "That's a *title*. What is God's *name*?" Many people will then answer, "Jesus!" whereupon the Witness will read John 4:23 and then comment, "You are not a true worshiper, because you are worshiping the Son. The Bible says here that the true worshipers will worship 'the Father.' Do you know the Father's name?" Then JW's proceed to present their standard argument about the name *Jehovah*.

Much of the Witnesses' preaching activity follows this same theme: denying the deity of Christ, while teaching that only the Father *(Jehovah)* must be worshiped. To establish this doctrine, they take their new students on a guided tour through the Bible, studiously avoiding such passages as Isaiah 9:6; Matthew 28:9; John 1:1; John 8:58–59; John 20:28; Colossians 2:9; Hebrews 1:6; and so on—all of which reveal the deity of Christ and the propriety of worshiping him.

In fact, Watchtower Society translators, in preparing their *New World Translation,* were careful to translate the Greek word *proskuneo* (worship, reverence, do obeisance to) in a very selective manner. Wherever the word is used of the Father, they translate it as "worship," but wherever it refers to the Son, they render it as "do obeisance to." (See discussion of Heb. 1:6 for further details.)

After agreeing that the Father should be worshiped, ask the Jehovah's Witness if he respects the Father's wishes in other matters, too. Naturally, he will answer, "Yes!" Then direct him in his own Bible to John 5:23, where it says that the Father requires "that all may honor the Son just as they honor the Father. . . ." If the Witness does not give worshipful honor to the Son, then his worship of the Father is in vain, because the same verse goes on to read: "He that does not honor the Son does not honor the Father who sent him."

See also Genesis 18:1–2; Exodus 3:14; Psalm 110:1; Isaiah 9:6; Daniel 10:13, 21; and Hebrews 1:6.

John 6:53

> Accordingly Jesus said to them: "Most truly I say to you, Unless you eat the flesh of the Son of man and drink his blood, you have no life in yourselves." (NWT)

This is an important verse to bring up in a discussion with Jehovah's Witnesses. They have been taught not only to reject taking communion but also to reject the new life that comes to all who put faith in the shed blood and crucified body of our Lord. They exclude themselves from the New Covenant ratified by the blood of Christ.

For suggestions on how to discuss this with them, see Matthew 26:27 and Revelation 7:9.

John 8:58

> Jesus said to them, "Truly, truly, I say to you, before Abraham
> was, I am." (RSV)

To avoid the obvious implication regarding the deity of
Christ, Watchtower translators changed Jesus' words in
their *New World Translation* to read: "Before Abraham
came into existence, I have been."

See our discussion of Exodus 3:14, where God revealed
himself to Moses as the "I AM."

John 10:16

> "And other sheep I have which are not of this fold; them also
> I must bring, and they will hear My voice; and there will be one
> flock and one shepherd." (NKJV)

If Jesus was here calling the future Gentile believers
his "other sheep," as is commonly understood, then he was
hinting to his Jewish disciples about the time when his
flock would embrace a worldwide body of believers from
all nationalities. But the Watchtower Society attaches a
different meaning to this text. They contrast the "other
sheep" with the "little flock" mentioned at Luke 12:32,
where the Lord said, "Do not fear, little flock, for it is your
Father's good pleasure to give you the kingdom" (NKJV).
The "little flock," Witnesses say, are 144,000 spirit-anointed
believers who make up the body of Christ and will go to
heaven, while the "other sheep" include all other believers—those who will receive everlasting life on earth. The
opportunity to become part of the "little flock" ended back
in the year 1935, so their story goes; thus, better than 99
percent of the Jehovah's Witnesses today consider themselves to be of the "other sheep" class.

This matter might almost seem academic, except for the
fact that those who see themselves as "other sheep" thereby

exclude themselves not only from heaven, but also from the New Covenant mediated by Christ and from all that the Bible promises to members of the body of Christ.

To refute the doctrine that Christians are divided into heavenly and earthly classes, see the discussions at Revelation 7:4 (about the "little flock" of 144,000) and Revelation 7:9 (about the "great crowd" of "other sheep").

Besides the vast majority of JW's, the Watchtower Society also throws all pre-Christian believers into the "other sheep" class with an earthly hope. Thus, Witnesses believe that Abraham, Isaac, Jacob, the prophets, and so on, do not go to heaven. The best response to this is to read the eleventh chapter of Hebrews, which refers to several faithful pre-Christian men and women (including the patriarchs and the prophets) and then says of them that "they were strangers and exiles on the earth. . . . But as it is, they desire a better country, that is, a heavenly one. Therefore God . . . has prepared for them a city" (Heb. 11:13, 16, RSV). What city in a heavenly country? Evidently, the "city of the living God, the heavenly Jerusalem" (Heb. 12:22, RSV).

See also the discussions of Psalm 37:9, 11, 29; Psalm 115:16; Matthew 23:43; and Revelation 7:9.

John 14:28

". . . If ye loved me, ye would rejoice, because I said, I go unto the Father: for my Father is greater than I." (KJV)

This is a favorite verse for Jehovah's Witnesses arguing against the deity of Christ. They begin by quoting from the Athanasian Creed: "And in this Trinity none is afore, or after an other; none is greater, or less than another. But the whole three persons are co-eternal, and co-equal." Then they will read Jesus' words about the Father being *greater* than the Son, rather than "equal," as that creed says.

John 14:28

Don't let JW's lure you into this trap. Remind them that Jesus was speaking at a time when he had done as stated at Philippians 2:6–7: "Who, being in the form of God, thought it not robbery to be equal with God: But made himself of no reputation, and took upon him the form of a servant, and was made in the likeness of men" (KJV). Naturally, then, Christ could speak of the Father as being "greater than I." The Son had even become "lower than the angels," in order to act as the Savior of mankind (Heb. 2:9).

See also the discussions of Isaiah 9:6; John 1:1; John 20:28; and Revelation 1:7–8.

John 16:13

"However, when He, the Spirit of truth, has come, He will guide you into all truth; for He will not speak on His own authority, but whatever He hears He will speak; and He will tell you things to come." (NKJV)

The whole series of verses at John 16:7–15 is an excellent passage to turn to when discussing the Holy Spirit with Jehovah's Witnesses. The JW's deny both the deity and the personality of the Holy Spirit, claiming instead that "it" is simply an impersonal "active force." But here Jesus plainly referred to the Holy Spirit as "He" (a personal pronoun) and described the Spirit as speaking, hearing, telling, and so on—activities of a clearly personal nature.

See also Genesis 1:1–2; Matthew 3:11; Acts 2:4; Acts 5:3–4; and 1 Corinthians 6:19.

John 17:3

"This means everlasting life, their taking in knowledge of you, the only true God, and of the one whom you sent forth, Jesus Christ." (NWT)

One of the verses most frequently quoted by door-knocking Jehovah's Witnesses is John 17:3. They use it in two different ways:

First, although most translations render the Greek as "to know" God, the Watchtower version says "taking in knowledge." This enables Witnesses to use the verse in offering listeners a "free home Bible study" in order to take in this so-called knowledge of God. Those who accept the offer are quickly switched from the Bible to one of the many books published by the Watchtower Bible and Tract Society.

After that, the persons studying with the Witnesses are "Ever learning, and never able to come to the knowledge of the truth" (2 Tim. 3:7, KJV). Jesus Christ himself revealed that he *is* "the Way and the Truth and the Life," and that "no one comes to the Father except through Me" (John 14:6, MLB). The "facts" that keep filling Witnesses' heads never make up for the lack of actually *knowing* Jesus, the living Truth.

It is like the situation of a young fan of a famous movie star who has seen all the star's movies, read volumes of biographical material, and decorated his walls with the star's pictures. Yet all of this knowledge can never add up to the sort of relationship enjoyed by the star's adopted son, who lives in a close relationship with him. Real Christianity involves being adopted by God as his child, and really coming to *know* him (see Gal. 4:5–9; Rom. 8:14–39). Watchtower-supplied "knowledge" can never equal that.

The second way that Jehovah's Witnesses use John 17:3 is to deny the deity of Christ. They point out that Jesus called the Father "the only true God" and made a distinction between "you, the only true God" *and* "the one whom you sent forth, Jesus Christ." Of course, the relationship of Father, Son, and Holy Spirit within the Godhead is a matter that even orthodox Christians can at best "see through a glass, darkly," while we look forward to

81

going home to be with the Lord and, only then, seeing him "face to face" (1 Cor. 13:12, KJV). But, we can see clearly enough right now to know that the Watchtower Society is twisting John 17:3.

If Jesus' reference to the Father as "the only true God" were meant to exclude the Son from deity, then the same principle of interpretation would have to apply to Jude 4, where Jesus Christ is called "our *only* Owner and Lord" (NWT, italics added). This would have to exclude the Father from Lordship and Ownership. Yet, Witnesses speak of the Father as "the Lord Jehovah," even though Jude 4 calls Jesus our "only" Lord. And the Holy Spirit is called "Lord" at 2 Corinthians 3:17. Obviously, then, neither use of the word *only* is exclusive with reference to the Father, the Son, and the Holy Spirit. Jesus' being called our "only" Lord does not rule out the Lordship of the Father and the Holy Spirit, and the Father's being called the "only" true God does not exclude the Son and the Holy Spirit from deity.

See also the discussions of Genesis 18:1–2; Exodus 3:14; Psalm 110:1; Isaiah 9:6; John 1:1; John 20:28; and Revelation 1:7–8.

John 20:25

> Consequently the other disciples would say to him: "We have seen the Lord!" But he said to them: "Unless I see in his hands the print of the nails and stick my finger into the print of the nails and stick my hand into his side, I will certainly not believe." (NWT)

Christians do well to discuss this passage with Jehovah's Witnesses who deny that Jesus died on a cross.

That Jesus did not die on a cross is a basic JW doctrine. In fact, Witnesses consider anyone who believes in the cross to be a "pagan false religionist." Instead, the Watchtower Society teaches that Jesus was nailed to a "torture stake"—an upright pole, like a flagpole, without any cross beam. Wherever other Bibles have the word *cross,* the *New World Translation* substitutes the expression *torture stake.*

Illustrations of the Lord's death in their books show Jesus with his arms brought together straight above his head, with a single nail pinning both hands to the stake. For years, all the Watchtower Society's publications have depicted Jesus' death in this way—with a *single nail* pinning his hands to a "torture stake." But, what does Scripture say? Did *one* nail fasten Jesus' hands above his head, or did *two* nails hold his hands to the opposite ends of a cross beam? At John 20:25, the Bible tells us that the apostle Thomas said the above. Even in the Watchtower Bible, Thomas spoke of the "nails" (plural) in Jesus' hands—not a single nail, as in Watchtower illustrations.

So, although JW leaders took out the word *cross* from their Bible, they neglected to take out the second nail in Jesus' hands—thus retaining evidence that he died by crucifixion, rather than the stake-*fiction* that they teach.

John 20:28

In answer Thomas said to him: "My Lord and my God!" (NWT)

Yes, this verse actually appears in the Jehovah's Witness Bible! Perhaps it will be changed in a future edition, but, while it is still there, we can point it out to JW's in conversations about the deity of Christ. Thomas, although doubting longer than the other apostles, finally came to accept Christ as Lord and God—not "a god" as Watchtower leaders have mistranslated John 1:1 to read in their Bible, but "God," as his words show.

Jehovah's Witnesses find this verse very difficult to deal with because they do not want to admit the simple fact that it declares Christ's deity. Typically, they try to cope with it in one of two ways:

First, the less knowledgeable JW may try to brush it off by saying, "Thomas was just exclaiming his surprise. If we saw a friend return from the dead, we, too, might say, 'Oh! My God!' out of sheer surprise. Thomas didn't mean anything by it."

If a Witness takes this approach, we should ask him, "Do you mean that Thomas was using God's name in vain? That would be blasphemy! Thomas certainly wouldn't do that." Then point out that in the next verse Jesus commented on what Thomas has said. If Thomas had said "God" in vain, Jesus would surely have rebuked him for it, but, instead, he acknowledged that Thomas had finally "believed." Believed what? That Jesus Christ is both Lord and God!

Second, the more sophisticated Witness will follow the approach suggested on page 213 of the Watchtower Society's 1985 book *Reasoning from the Scriptures.* He will point out that the twentieth chapter of John ends by saying that "these have been written down that you may believe that Jesus is the Christ the Son of God . . ." (v. 31). To the JW, the fact that the Father is God, and Jesus is the Son of the Father, automatically rules out the Son's deity. But this is not what Scripture teaches. (See verses listed below.) The Witness may also quote John 20:17, where Jesus refers to the Father as "my God," as so-called proof that Jesus is not God. Yet, at Hebrews 1:10, the Father calls the Son "Lord"—obviously without casting doubt on the fact that the Father, too, is "Lord."

Since the Witnesses refer to Jesus as "a god" in contrast with the Father, whom they call "the God," you may wish to have the JW look up John 20:28 in his own *Kingdom Interlinear* (1985) Bible. The word-for-word English under the Greek text shows that Thomas literally called Jesus, "The Lord of me and *the God* of me!"

See also Genesis 18:1–2; Isaiah 9:6; Daniel 10:13, 21;

12:1; John 1:1; Revelation 1:7–8; and other pertinent verses listed in the Subject-Matter Index.

Acts

Acts 1:5

"For John baptized with water, but in a few days you will be baptized with the Holy Spirit." (NIV)

See discussion of the same thought at Matthew 3:11.

Acts 2:4

. . . they all became filled with holy spirit. . . . (NWT)

The Watchtower's 1982 book *You Can Live Forever in Paradise on Earth* says: " 'They all became filled with holy spirit.' (Acts 2:4) Were they 'filled' with a person? No, but they were filled with God's active force. Thus the facts make clear that the Trinity is not a Bible teaching. . . . How could the holy spirit be a person, when it filled about 120 disciples at the same time?" (pp. 40–41). And the study question at the bottom of page 41 asks, "How does the pouring out of holy spirit on Jesus' followers prove that it is not a person?"

These Jehovah's Witness arguments do not prove anything of the sort. If the *pouring out* of the Holy Spirit (Acts 2:33; 10:45; and so on) were evidence against personality, then the apostle Paul would not be a person either, because Paul wrote concerning himself: "I am being poured out . . ." (Phil. 2:17, NWT) and: ". . . I am already being poured out . . ." (2 Tim. 4:6, NWT). Since the apostle Paul, obviously a real person, could be spoken of in the Bible as being "poured out," then the use of the same expression with regard to the Holy Spirit could hardly be used as a proof against the Spirit's personality.

85

Likewise, the Old Testament prophecy says of Jesus Christ, "like water I have been poured out" (Ps. 22:14, NWT). Therefore, applying the Watchtower argument would make him a mere impersonal force also. Clearly, the argument is a fallacy.

But what about the matter of the disciples being "filled" with the Holy Spirit? Rather than supporting what Jehovah's Witnesses believe, this verse actually proves the opposite: namely, that the Holy Spirit is the Lord God himself. He is the One who "fills all in all" (Eph. 1:23, RSV), "Him who fills all in all" (NKJV). Even the JW *New World Translation* refers to "him who fills up all things in all" at Ephesians 1:23. Ask the Jehovah's Witness if this "him" who fills all the disciples is not a divine person.

Next show the Witness that the Holy Spirit can speak (Acts 13:2), bear witness (John 15:26), "say whatever He hears" (John 16:13, MLB), and "feel hurt" (Isa. 63:10, NWT).

Finally, ask the Witness to read 2 Corinthians 3:17. Most translations of that verse say, "the Lord is the Spirit." The Watchtower's Bible says, "Jehovah is the Spirit." Clearly the Scriptures teach that the Holy Spirit is a divine person—none other than God himself.

See also the discussions of Matthew 3:11; John 16:3; Acts 5:3–4; and 1 Corinthians 6:19.

Acts 5:3–4

> But Peter said, "Ananias, why has Satan filled your heart to lie to the Holy Spirit and keep back part of the price of the land for yourself? . . . You have lied not to men but to God." (NKJV)

Invite a Jehovah's Witness to read this passage; then ask him to whom it was that Ananias lied. Peter mentions it twice: he lied to the Holy Spirit; he lied to God. This reveals that the Holy Spirit is a person—(How could someone lie to a "force"?)—and that this person is God.

You may have to read this passage a couple of times

with the Witness before he even begins to grasp the point. JW's are so accustomed to thinking of the Holy Spirit as an "it"—"Jehovah's active force"—that their minds have difficulty even formulating the thought of the Holy Spirit as a person.

One passage will not be enough to convince the Witness of the personality and deity of the Holy Spirit. See also our discussions of John 16:13; Romans 8:26–27; and 1 Corinthians 6:19. The Witness may still object to the Spirit's personality, saying that the Holy Spirit can be "poured out," and that people can be "filled" and "baptized" with the Holy Spirit. If those objections are raised, please see our discussions of Matthew 3:11 and Acts 2:4.

Acts 7:59–60

> While they were stoning him, Stephen prayed, "Lord Jesus, receive my spirit." Then he fell on his knees and cried out, "Lord, do not hold this sin against them. . . ." (NIV)

Jehovah's Witnesses *never* address Jesus in prayer. They have been taught that their prayers must be directed only to the Father and that they must call him "Jehovah." If a Witness were overheard praying to Jesus, he would be put on trial by a judicial committee and would be disfellowshiped unless he repented of his "sin."

But the Scripture passage above clearly shows Stephen praying to Jesus Christ, the risen Lord. (The JW Bible changes "Lord" in v. 60 to "Jehovah," but v. 59 still says "Jesus.")

A Witness may try to claim that Stephen was not praying to Jesus; he was merely speaking to him face to face, because he saw him in a vision. In that case, ask the JW to read the context. The vision in verse 56 took place when Stephen was in Jerusalem, standing trial before the Jewish Sanhedrin court. When he told the Jews that he saw a vision of Christ in heaven at the right hand of the

Father, they were filled with fury. They ended the trial, dragged Stephen out of the court chamber, led him through the city streets, took him all the way out of the city (v. 57), and then stoned him. This naturally took a considerable amount of time. There is no indication that Stephen's vision was repeated again outside the city at the time of his stoning. Rather, he was, as the Scripture states, praying to Jesus.

Acts 15:28-29

> For it seemed good to the Holy Ghost, and to us, to lay upon you no greater burden than these necessary things; That ye abstain from meats offered to idols, and from blood, and from things strangled, and from fornication: from which if ye keep yourselves, ye shall do well. (KJV)

Jehovah's Witnesses use this verse, along with Old Testament dietary regulations, to support their organization's ban on blood transfusions.

They see the above passage as a law from God, extending the Jewish dietary prohibition on blood to the Christian congregation for all time to come. But did the early church treat this apostolic letter as a permanent injunction? Obviously, fornication is permanently forbidden, but what about the other things mentioned in the letter? What about meats offered to idols? Paul discussed this subject at greater length in his first letter to the Corinthians, pointing out that "an idol is nothing" and that "neither, if we eat, are we the better; neither, if we eat not, are we the worse." He urged against eating such meat in cases where it might become a stumbling block to new believers who had only recently abandoned idolatrous worship. (See 1 Cor. 8:1-13, KJV.) But, in general, Christians were free to "Eat whatever is sold in the [pagan] meat market without raising any question on the ground of conscience" and to "eat whatever is set before you" in a pagan neighbor's home (1 Cor. 10:25, 27, RSV).

Therefore, the part of the letter of Acts 15 that refers to meats offered to idols must *not* have been viewed as a permanent injunction for the church. There is no basis, then, for claiming that the statement about blood has force today either.

But, even if it did, the Scripture is still talking about *diet,* not blood transfusions. To take a dietary regulation and stretch it to the point of denying a lifesaving medical procedure to a dying man is reminiscent of the Jewish Pharisees who were furious when Jesus healed a man on the Sabbath (Luke 6:6–11). A letter published in the December 8, 1984, issue of *The Concord Monitor* (New Hampshire) tells of Jehovah's Witness elders interrogating a terminal cancer patient in a hospital and then disfellowshiping him on his deathbed because he accepted a blood transfusion. We could easily picture the Pharisees doing the same thing—but would Jesus act like that?

See also the discussions at Genesis 9:4 and Leviticus 7:26–27.

Romans

Romans 8:8–9

> . . . and those who are in the flesh cannot please God. But you are not in the flesh, you are in the Spirit, if the Spirit of God really dwells in you. Any one who does not have the Spirit of Christ does not belong to him. (RSV)

This passage is very helpful in showing Jehovah's Witnesses their need to be born again as children of God. They hope to please God by the works that they are busy doing. But they are still in the flesh, and, therefore, "cannot please God," no matter how many good works they do.

Beginning at verse one, read through Romans 8 with

the JW, especially up to and including verse seventeen. For help in doing this, see our discussion of John 3:3.

Romans 8:26–27

> Likewise the Spirit also helps in our weaknesses. For we do not know what we should pray for as we ought, but the Spirit Himself makes intercession for us with groanings which cannot be uttered. And He who searches the hearts knows what the mind of the Spirit is, because He makes intercession for the saints according to the will of God. (NKJV)

Jehovah's Witnesses seldom encounter this passage in their organized "Bible studies" because their leaders prefer to skip over or ignore it. It just does not fit in with their conception of the Holy Spirit as an "it"—an impersonal "active force."

Invite the JW to read these verses with you, and then ask him some pointed questions: Can a "force" make intercession for us? Does a "force" have a mind? The Witnesses' own *New World Translation* says that the Spirit "pleads for us" (v. 26). Can an impersonal force plead for people?

To help the Witness reason further on the personality and deity of the Holy Spirit, invite him to consider also John 16:13; Acts 5:3–4; and 1 Corinthians 6:19. (See discussions of those verses.)

Romans 14:7–9

> None of us lives to himself, and none of us dies to himself. If we live, we live to the Lord, and if we die, we die to the Lord, so then, whether we live or whether we die, we are the Lord's. For to this end Christ died and lived again, that he might be Lord both of the dead and of the living. (RSV)

This is an excellent example to cite when demonstrating that the Jehovah's Witnesses' *New World Translation* of the Bible is a twisted translation, containing numerous verses that have been changed to fit Watchtower doctrines.

As it reads in the above Revised Standard Version and in virtually every other translation, this passage shows our relationship to Christ both in life and in death. Verse 9 is logically connected to what precedes it in verses 7 and 8. But, now, note how Watchtower translators have changed the verse in their Bible:

> None of us, in fact, lives with regard to himself only, and no one dies with regard to himself only; for both if we live, we live to Jehovah, and if we die, we die to Jehovah. Therefore both if we live and if we die, we belong to Jehovah. For to this end Christ died and came to life again, that he might be Lord over both the dead and the living (Rom. 14:7-9, NWT).

By rendering the same Greek root *Kyrios* as "Jehovah" in verses 7 and 8, and as "Lord" in verse 9, the Watchtower has created a logical *non sequitur*—verse 9 no longer follows logically from the preceding thought. Remembering that the JW leaders teach that "Jehovah" is the name of God the Father only, and that Jesus Christ is a mere created being (an angel), we see that they have totally changed the thought of this passage. In their rendering, the subject of the discussion changes from God to one of his creatures as you read from verse 8 to verse 9, and so verse 9 is no longer logically tied in with what precedes it. You don't have to be a Greek scholar to see that something is wrong with the Watchtower Society's rendering of this passage.

In the Jehovah's Witness Bible it appears that two different persons are spoken of in Romans 14:7-9. Yet a quick glance at the Watchtower's own *Kingdom Interlinear Translation* shows that the same root word, *Kyrios* ("Lord"), appears in all three verses. In order to be consistent, the English rendering should reflect this by using "Lord" throughout the discussion.

But why did the Watchtower Society's translators not render *Kyrios* as "Jehovah" in all three verses? Because then it would read: "None of us, in fact, lives with regard to himself only, and no one dies with regard to himself only; for both if we live, we live to Jehovah, and if we die, we die to Jehovah. Therefore both if we live and if we die, we belong to Jehovah. For to this end Christ died and came to life again, that he might be Jehovah over both the dead and the living"—a thought totally unacceptable in Watchtower theology!

In many other ways, too, the *New World Translation* twists verses to fit the organization's doctrines. Instead of being called the Watchtower's version of the Bible, it should be called their *per*version of the Bible.

See also our chapter two, "The Bible That Jehovah's Witnesses Use."

First Corinthians

1 Corinthians 1:10

> Now I beseech you, brethren, by the name of our Lord Jesus Christ, that ye all speak the same thing, and that there be no divisions among you; but that ye be perfectly joined together in the same mind and in the same judgment. (KJV)

The Watchtower Society uses this verse to impose upon its followers a degree of lockstep conformity that is incredible to outsiders. And, rather than chafe under it, Witnesses actually boast of their total obedience to the Society as evidence that they are the only true Christians, because they alone "all speak in agreement" and are "united in the same mind and in the same line of thought" (1 Cor. 1:10, NWT).

They are specifically instructed not to accept or *read* "the religious literature of people they meet" (*The Watchtower*, 5/1/84, p. 31), not to *listen* to "criticism of Jehovah's organization" (*The Watchtower,* 5/15/84, p. 17), and not to *speak* words "expressing criticism of the way the appointed elders are handling matters" (*The Watchtower,* 1/15/84, p. 16). The Witnesses are even told to "Avoid independent thinking . . . questioning the counsel that is provided by God's visible organization," and to "Fight against independent thinking" (*The Watchtower,* 1/15/83, pp. 22, 27).

But did the apostle Paul, in writing to the Corinthians, mean that they should not only end their schismatic divisions but should also submit themselves to some human leader in total, unquestioning obedience—like mindless robots? Hardly! Paul's further writings to the Romans reveal that there was plenty of room for individual freedom in the early church:

> People range from those who believe they may eat any sort of meat to those whose faith is so weak they dare not eat anything except vegetables. Meat-eaters must not condemn the scrupulous. On the other hand, the scrupulous must not condemn those who feel free to eat anything they choose, since God has welcomed them. . . . If one man keeps certain days as holier than others, and another considers all days to be equally holy, each must be left free to hold his own opinion (Rom. 14:2–5, JB).

As Christians, we should certainly be united on the basics of our faith, all of us joining together in following Christ as Lord and looking to him as our Savior, but there is also room for diversity. We might even disagree on matters that would necessitate meeting separately from those of another opinion. For example, it would be difficult for meat-eaters and vegetarians to share a banquet together, and those who do not observe a particular "holy day" would normally not attend a service that others held to celebrate it. But such disagreements should not be allowed to break the bond of love that unites us as brothers and sisters in

Christ. Even if our brother feels differently on such matters, we should "welcome him all the same without starting an argument" (Rom. 14:1, JB). Point out to the Jehovah's Witness that it is not lockstep conformity, but *love,* that is "a perfect bond of union" (Col. 3:14, NWT).

In reasoning on the matter with a Witness, you might freely admit that Christians regret the divisions that plague the church. Some of these are due to traditions that developed over the centuries in different localities due to geographical separation and language barriers. Others are the result of sincere differences of opinion among men who equally respect the Bible and accept the Lordship of Christ, but who have reached different conclusions in areas where Scripture speaks ambiguously or not at all. The solution, however, does not lie in one organization's leaders standing up and announcing to the world: "Everyone must agree with *us*! Then we will all be of 'one mind' as true Christians." That approach has been tried many times, and it leads only to deeper divisions. In fact, there are numerous exclusivist religious groups that claim to be "the only true Christians," the Watchtower Society being only one among many. Finding those who agree with you, and then disfellowshiping the rest of the world, is not the way to true Christian unity.

The Jehovah's Witness should also be asked to look at one area in which the Watchtower Society specifically violates scriptural admonition. This is the matter of holidays, or holy days. As we noted above, Romans 14:5-6 makes allowance for individual Christians to observe special days that other Christians may choose not to observe. Yet the JW who dares to celebrate Christmas or Easter or Thanksgiving Day (or even Mother's Day!) is immediately put on trial by a judicial committee and disfellowshiped—totally cut off from friends and family.

For further discussion of Jehovah's Witness' conformity to instructions from the Watchtower organization, see Matthew 24:45 and Revelation 19:1.

1 Corinthians 6:19

Do you not know that your body is a temple of the Holy
Spirit, who is in you, whom you have received from God? . . .

Here is a line of reasoning to use with a Jehovah's
Witness, when presenting the deity of the Holy Spirit:

Besides the temple of the True God in ancient Jerusalem, the Scriptures mention many other temples—for
example: the temple of Dagon (1 Sam. 5:2), the temple of
Zeus (Acts 14:13), the temple of Artemis (Acts 19:35), and
so on. Each one was *someone's* temple, either the True
God's or a false God's. But the Bible also shows that the
physical body of each individual Christian becomes a
temple. Whose temple? A "temple of the Holy Spirit"
(1 Cor. 6:19).

Not recognizing the Holy Spirit as a person, namely
God himself, followers of the Watchtower find it impossible to grasp this teaching of Scripture: that God becomes
personally present within each believer. Yet, their own
Kingdom Interlinear Translation's literal word-for-word
rendering of the Greek at 1 Corinthians 6:19 says: ". . .
the body of you divine habitation of the in you holy spirit
is. . . ." Obviously, these words indicate that the Holy Spirit
is divine and that he inhabits Christians.

The promise of this wonderful, close relationship with
God was given by Jesus, when he said: ". . . I shall ask the
Father and He will give you another Helper to stay with
you forever, the Spirit of Truth. . . . You know Him, for He
remains with you and will be within you" (John 14:16, 17,
MLB). Pray that the Jehovah's Witnesses may come to know
God in this intimate way.

See also the discussions of John 16:13 and Acts 5:3–4.

1 Corinthians 8:6

But to us there is but one God, the Father, of whom are all
things, and we in him; and one Lord Jesus Christ, by whom are
all things, and we by him. (KJV)

"There is but one God," says the Jehovah's Witness in applying this verse, "and who is he? The Father! So, Jesus is not God." However, there is a flaw in his line of reasoning. Don't let him stop there; make him apply the same line of reasoning to the rest of the verse. Then he will have to say, "There is but one Lord, and who is he? Jesus Christ! So, the Father is not Lord." Of course, the JW does not want to reach this conclusion, because he always speaks of Jehovah as "Lord." Point out to him that he cannot have the one without the other. He cannot make the first half of the verse exclude Jesus from being God, without making the second half exclude the Father from being Lord.

The fact is that Scripture uses the terms *God* and *Lord* virtually interchangeably. The various false gods are called both "gods" and "lords." The Father is called both "God" and "Lord," and the Son is referred to by both terms. The apostle Thomas addressed Jesus as "my Lord and my God" (John 20:28). Watchtower leaders have taught their disciples to see in 1 Corinthians 8:6 a contrast that does not exist.

See also the discussions of Isaiah 9:6; John 1:1; John 17:3; John 20:28; and Revelation 1:7–8.

1 Corinthians 11:3

> But I would have you know, that the head of every man is Christ; and the head of the woman is the man; and the head of Christ is God. (KJV)

Jehovah's Witnesses use this verse, too, in their attempt to deny the deity of Christ. But this passage does not support Watchtower doctrine that Christ was an angel created by God. It simply shows that the principle of *headship* applies.

Within the human family, the head of the woman is the man. Does that mean that women are a lower form of life than men? Are women somehow inferior to men? Not at all! It is simply God's arrangement that someone act as head, and he assigned that role to the man. Likewise within the Godhead—the Father acts as head without diminishing the full deity of the Son.

See also our discussion of Isaiah 9:6; John 1:1; John 20:28; Colossians 2:9; and Revelation 1:7–8.

Colossians

Colossians 1:15

> He is the image of the invisible God, the first-born of all creation. (RSV)

Jehovah's Witnesses cite this verse as "proof" that Jesus Christ is not God, but rather the first angel that God created. However, does the word *first-born* in the Bible necessarily mean the first one who was born or created? Not at all! The term is often used in Scripture to signify priority in importance or rank, rather than actual birth order.

For example, ask the Witness to turn to Psalm 89:27. This verse speaks about King David, who was the youngest, or *last*-born son of Jesse—as far away as he could be from being literally first-born. But note what God says about him in the psalm: "Also, I myself shall place him as firstborn . . ." (NWT). Clearly, God did not reverse the order of David's birth; he was not speaking about birth order. What the psalm meant was that King David would be elevated in rank, above the others, to the preeminent position.

Now, to demonstrate that the term is used in this sense when speaking about Christ at Colossians 1:15, ask the Witness to look at the context. Point out, particularly, verse 18, which identifies Christ as "the head" and "the first-born" and says that this is for the purpose "that in everything he might be pre-eminent" (RSV).

While you are right there in the Book of Colossians,

clinch the point about the deity of Christ by reading chapter 2, verse 9: "For in Christ all the fullness of the Deity lives in bodily form" (NIV).

See also the discussions of Isaiah 9:6; Daniel 10:13, 21; 12:1; John 1:1; John 20:28; Revelation 1:7–8; and other verses listed in the Subject-Matter Index.

Colossians 2:9

For in Christ all the fullness of the Deity lives in bodily form. (NIV)

This is a text that should definitely be included when sharing with a Jehovah's Witness the abundant scriptural evidence that Jesus Christ is God. Reading it in a number of translations may prove helpful: "For in him dwelleth all the fulness of the Godhead bodily" (KJV). "For in Christ there is all of God in a human body" (LB) and "in him all the fullness of deity is resident in bodily form" (*The Bible in Living English,* translated by Steven T. Byington, published by the Watchtower Society, 1972).

The Watchtower's *New World Translation* attempts to water down the message of this verse by rendering it: "because it is in him that all the fullness of the divine quality dwells bodily." But the reference edition (footnote) and the interlinear version of their Bible both admit that the Greek word they translate as "divine quality" literally means "godship."

See also the discussions of Isaiah 9:6; John 1:1; John 20:28; Revelation 1:7–8; and other related references listed in the Subject-Matter Index.

2 Timothy 3:16—17

All Scripture is inspired of God and beneficial for teaching, for reproving, for setting things straight, for disciplining in righteousness, that the man of God may be fully competent, completely equipped for every good work. (NWT)

Jehovah's Witnesses will express strong agreement with this passage. In fact, they quote it quite often. But, in practice, they don't really believe the latter half of it. They don't believe that a man of God is fully competent and completely equipped, unless he has their organization's books and magazines. The Bible alone is not enough.

We Christians also have Christian magazines, books, concordances, Bible dictionaries, and so on. We see this literature as helpful and instructive, but we don't feel that we *need* these supplements in order to understand the gospel message, come into God's favor, and gain eternal life. In fact, testimonies are often told of individuals who— through reading the Bible alone—have come into a saving relationship with Jesus Christ.

Jehovah's Witnesses, on the other hand, believe that one must have their organization's literature in order to be saved. In commenting on the Society's own *Scripture Studies* books, *The Watch Tower* (9/15/10, p. 298) said:

> Furthermore, not only do we find that people cannot see the divine plan in studying the Bible by itself, but we see, also, that if anyone lays the *Scripture Studies* aside . . . and goes to the Bible alone, though he has understood his Bible for ten years, our experience shows that within two years he goes into darkness. On the other hand, if he had merely read the *Scripture Studies* with their references, and had not read a page of the Bible, as such, he would be in the light at the end of the two years.

Have Jehovah's Witnesses of today abandoned that view expressed in the words of their organization's founder, Charles Taze Russell, back in 1910? Compare that quote with this more recent statement in *The Watchtower* (12/1/81, p. 27):

> But Jehovah God has also provided his visible organization, his "faithful and discreet slave," made up of spirit-anointed ones, to help Christians in all nations to understand and apply properly the Bible in their lives. Unless

we are in touch with this channel of communication that God is using, we will not progress along the road to life, no matter how much Bible reading we do.

The thought is the same! The inspired Scriptures alone do *not* make a person "fully competent and completely equipped" (2 Tim. 3:17) in the eyes of Jehovah's Witnesses.

What happens if a JW *does* read the Bible alone, without Watchtower Society books and magazines? The organization made an amazing admission about this, when it stated the following about ex-members:

> They say that it is sufficient to read the Bible exclusively, either alone or in small groups at home. But, strangely, through such "Bible reading," they have reverted right back to the apostate doctrines that commentaries by Christendom's clergy were teaching 100 years ago. . . [*The Watchtower,* 8/15/81, pp. 28–29].

So, the Watchtower Society itself admits that Jehovah's Witnesses who begin reading the Bible alone stop believing Watchtower doctrines and return to the doctrines taught in Christian churches. Whose doctrines, then, are the ones that are truly based on the Bible? The answer is obvious, by the Society's own admission.

Hebrews 1:6

But when he again brings his First-born into the inhabited earth, he says: "And let all God's angels worship him." (NWT, editions of 1953, 1960, 1961, and 1970)

When the editions of the Watchtower Bible cited above were printed, somehow this reference to worshiping Jesus Christ managed to escape the censor's knife. Every other mention of worshiping him was removed from the *New World Translation,* except this one that remained—but not for long! Beginning with the 1971 revision, all future editions were changed to read: "And let all God's angels do obeisance to him."

100

The context of this verse is most significant. The entire first chapter of Hebrews is devoted to contrasting Jesus Christ with the angels—showing the superiority of the Son of God over the angelic creation. But the Watchtower Society teaches that Jesus Christ *is* an angel. No wonder they changed verse six to eliminate the thought of worshiping him!

The Greek root here is *proskuneo,* which can properly be translated either "worship" or "obeisance," depending on the context and, in this case, the translator's bias. Invite the JW to turn to Revelation 22:8–9 in his own *Kingdom Interlinear Translation,* where the same word *proskuneo* is used in the original Greek. There the apostle John says, "I fell down to worship [root: *proskuneo*] before the feet of the angel. . . . But he tells me: 'Be careful! Do not do that! . . . Worship [root: *proskuneo*] God.' " Point out to the Jehovah's Witness that the worship that the *angel refused to accept,* but told John to give to God, is the same *proskuneo* that the Father commanded to be given to his Son Jesus at Hebrews 1:6. So, the Son is certainly not an angel.

Would it be appropriate to give the Son the same worshipful honor that is given to the Father? Let John 5:23 answer the question: "in order that all may honor the Son just as they honor the Father. He that does not honor the Son does not honor the Father who sent him" (NWT).

For further information on the deity of Christ and the propriety of worshiping him, see the discussions of Isaiah 9:6; Daniel 10:13, 21, 12:1; John 1:1; John 20:28; and other verses listed in the Subject-Matter Index.

Revelation

Revelation 1:7–8

Look! He is coming with the clouds, and every eye will see him, and those who pierced him; and all the tribes of the earth

will beat themselves in grief because of him. Yes, Amen. "I am
the Alpha and the Omega," says Jehovah God, "the One who is
and who was and who is coming, the Almighty." (NWT)

If Jesus Christ is shown to be "the Alpha and the
Omega" and "the First and the Last," while the JW Bible
also says that Jehovah God is "the Alpha and the Omega"
and "the First and the Last," the Jehovah's Witness must
either admit that Jesus Christ is the Almighty God—or
else close his eyes to the Word.

You might discuss these verses with a Witness as follows, using his own *New World Translation*:

Revelation 1:7–8, quoted above, says that someone
"is coming." Who? Verse 7 says it is someone who was
"pierced." Who was it that was pierced when he was nailed
up to die? Jesus! But verse 8 says that it is Jehovah God
who "is coming." Could it be that there are *two* who are
coming? No! Verse 8 refers to "the One who . . . is coming."

Revelation 1:8 states clearly that Jehovah God is the
Alpha and the Omega. Now note what he says at Reve-
lation 22:12–13: " 'Look! I am coming quickly . . . I am the
Alpha and the Omega, the first and the last. . . .' " So,
Jehovah God is coming quickly. But notice the response
when he says it again: " ' "Yes; I am coming quickly. "
Amen! Come, Lord Jesus' " (22:20, NWT).

At this point you might mention that *Alpha* is the
first letter of the Greek alphabet, while *Omega* is the last
letter. Therefore, "the Alpha and the Omega" means the
same thing as "the First and the Last." Then, again referring to the *New World Translation,* continue like this:

Who is speaking in Revelation 2:8? "These are the
things that he says, 'the First and the Last,' who became
dead and came to life again. . . ." Obviously, it is Jesus.
Who was Jesus identifying himself as being, when he
called himself "the First and the Last"? This is how Almighty God described himself in the Old Testament. Jesus
knew that the apostle John, who wrote the Revelation,
and later Bible readers would all remember these verses:

" '. . . I am the same One. I am the first. Moreover, I am the last. Moreover, my own hand laid the foundation of the earth, and my own right hand extended out the heavens . . .' " (Isa. 48:12–13). And: ". . . I am the same One. Before me there was no God formed, and after me there continued to be none. I—I am Jehovah, and besides me there is no savior" (Isa. 43:10–11).

Note, too, that the expression *the first and the last* is used this way to refer to the Jehovah God in Revelation 22:13: " 'I am the Alpha and the Omega, the first and the last, the beginning and the end.' " Yet John also records: ". . . . And he laid his right hand upon me and said: 'Do not be fearful. I am the First and the Last, and the living one; and I became dead, but look! I am living forever and ever . . .' " (Rev. 1:17–18).

Remind the Jehovah's Witness that he has read in his own Bible that Jehovah God is the One who is coming, the One who is coming quickly, the Alpha and the Omega, the First and the Last, and the only Savior. He has also read that our Savior Jesus Christ is the one who is coming, the One who is coming quickly, the Alpha and the Omega, the First and the Last.

If the Witness has difficulty reaching the right conclusion, namely that Jesus Christ *is* Almighty God, ask him to read Colossians 2:9: "it is in him that all the fullness of the divine quality dwells bodily" (NWT). Or, according to the New International Version, "For in Christ all the fullness of the Deity lives in bodily form."

See also the discussions of Genesis 18:1–2; Exodus 3:14; Isaiah 9:6; and John 1:1.

Revelation 3:14

> And unto the angel of the church of the Laodiceans write; These things saith the Amen, the faithful and true witness, the beginning of the creation of God. (KJV)

This verse is one of the Jehovah's Witnesses' favorites, in their attempt to "prove" that Jesus Christ is a mere created being, the first angel that God made. "Look!" they say. "Jesus is 'the beginning of the creation.' " But they should be careful. They will tell you that God the Father is the speaker at Revelation 21:6 and 22:13, yet in both verses he calls himself "the beginning." Therefore, "the beginning" must mean something else other than the first thing created.

Actually, in each of these cases, the Greek text says *archē*, a word listed in Vine's *Expository Dictionary of New Testament Words* as having such varied meanings as "beginning," "power," "magistrate," and "ruler." The Watchtower Bible translates the plural of the same word as "government officials" at Luke 12:11. It is the root of our words *archbishop, architect,* and other words referring to someone who is chief over others. Thus, the New International Version at Revelation 3:14 says that Christ is "the ruler of God's creation." So there is no basis for claiming that Revelation 3:14 makes Jesus Christ a created being.

See also Isaiah 9:6; John 1:1; John 20:28; and other verses cited in the Subject-Matter Index under "Jesus Christ."

Revelation 7:4

> And I heard the number of those who were sealed, a hundred and forty-four thousand, sealed out of every tribe of the sons of Israel. (NWT)

The Watchtower Society teaches that the Christian church, or body of Christ, is limited to a literal number of 144,000 individuals. This gathering of the 144,000 began at Pentecost in the first century and continued through the year 1935—at which time the number was completed and the door was closed. New believers since 1935 are not part of the congregation of 144,000, but form a secondary class called the "great crowd" of "other sheep." (See the discussion of Rev. 7:9 for further information on the "great crowd" and the 1935 date.) Since 1935, most of the remaining ones of the 144,000 have died off, leaving only about 9,000 alive on earth today—all of whom are Jehovah's Witnesses. Among the millions of JW's, only the remnant of the 144,000 have the hope of heaven, and only they may partake of the communion loaf and cup.

As with many of the symbolic word-pictures in the Book of Revelation, there is some debate even among true Christians as to just who the 144,000 may be. We can freely admit that to the Witnesses, while showing them that the Watchtower Society's interpretation is obviously wrong.

Revelation 7:4 says that the 144,000 are "of the sons of Israel," but the Watchtower Society teaches that the Christian congregation is here symbolically portrayed as "spiritual Israel," and that the 144,000 are therefore drawn from among all nations. We need only read the next few verses to discredit their interpretation: "Out of the tribe of Judah twelve thousand sealed; out of the tribe of Reuben twelve thousand; out of the tribe of Gad twelve thousand; out of the tribe of Asher twelve thousand; out of the tribe of Naphtali twelve thousand; out of the tribe of Manasseh twelve thousand; out of the tribe of Simeon twelve thousand; out of the tribe of Levi twelve thousand; out of the tribe of Issachar twelve thousand; out of the tribe of Zebulun twelve thousand; out of the tribe of Joseph twelve thousand; out of the tribe of Benjamin twelve thousand sealed" (Rev. 7:5–8, NWT). How more clearly could Israel be specified than by listing the twelve tribes making up that nation?

The Witnesses may respond by insisting that the references to 12,000 from each tribe are purely symbolic. But, if that is true, then the twelve symbolic numbers (12,000 + 12,000 + 12,000 + 12,000 + 12,000 + 12,000 + 12,000 + 12,000 + 12,000 + 12,000 + 12,000 + 12,000 = 144,000) must add up to a total that is also symbolic. Yet the Witnesses believe the 144,000 to be a literal number. So, again, their interpretation leads to a contradiction.

Revelation 7:9

> After these things I saw, and, look! a great crowd, which no man was able to number, out of all nations and tribes and peoples and tongues, standing before the throne and before the Lamb, dressed in white robes; and there were palm branches in their hands. (NWT)

The Watchtower Society teaches that in the year 1935 God stopped calling people to a heavenly hope in union with Christ. They say that in that year he began gathering a secondary class of believers, outside the body of Christ, whose hope would be to live forever on earth in the flesh. This class of people, they claim, is the "great crowd" of Revelation 7:9–17.

This is one of the most significant doctrines taught by the Watchtower Society. It forms the basis for convincing millions of Jehovah's Witnesses that:

1. They cannot become members of the body of Christ (1 Cor. 12:27).
2. They cannot be "born again" (John 3:3).
3. They cannot share in Christ's heavenly kingdom (2 Tim. 4:18).
4. They cannot receive the baptism of the Holy Spirit (1 Cor. 12:13).
5. They are not entitled to share in the communion loaf and cup (1 Cor. 10:16–17).
6. They are not in the New Covenant mediated by Christ (Heb. 12:24).
7. They cannot be fully justified through faith in Jesus Christ (Rom. 3:26).

Thus, the Society uses this "1935 doctrine" to deprive its followers of the relationship with God outlined in the New Testament for all believers.

Where does the Bible teach that entrance to the Christian congregation would be closed in the year 1935, with a secondary "great crowd" being gathered after that? Nowhere! Watchtower leaders claim that "light flashed up"—that Watchtower president J. F. Rutherford received a special "revelation of divine truth"—to introduce this change in 1935. They can produce *no scriptural support at all* for the 1935 date. Instead of turning to the Bible, they say:

> These flashes of prophetic light prepared the ground for the historic discourse on "The Great Multitude," given May 31, 1935, by the president of the Watch Tower Society, J. F. Rutherford, at the Washington, D.C., convention of Jehovah's Witnesses. What a revelation of divine truth that was! (*The Watchtower,* 3/1/85, p. 14, §12)
>
> . . . the heavenly hope was held out, highlighted and stressed until about the year 1935. Then as "light flashed up" to reveal clearly the identity of the "great crowd" of Revelation 7:9, the emphasis began to be placed on the earthly hope (*The Watchtower,* 2/1/82, p. 28, §16).

There is no biblical basis whatsoever for this teaching. Scripture discusses in detail the Old Covenant for the Jews and the New Covenant for Christians. But it makes no mention of any third arrangement for gathering a "great crowd" with an earthly hope after the year 1935.

Moreover, the verses the Witnesses cite in Revelation actually locate the "great crowd" as "before the throne and before the Lamb" (7:9, NWT), "before the throne of God" (7:15, NWT), and "in his temple" (7:15, NWT)—all *heavenly* locations, rather than on earth as the Watchtower Society teaches.

In fact, the reference to "a great crowd . . . crying with a loud voice, saying: 'Salvation we owe to our God . . .' " (7:9–10) is quite similar to the wording of the only other mention of "a great crowd" in the Watchtower's *New World*

Translation of the Book of Revelation. This is in chapter 19, where the invitation to "Be praising our God, all you his slaves, who fear him, the small ones and the great" is responded to by "a voice of a great crowd" (19:5–6). Yet the Scripture specifically says that it is "a loud voice of a great crowd *in heaven*" (v. 1, italics added).

Once the Watchtower Society's interpretation has been proved wrong, it is not necessary (or advisable) to get into a discussion with Jehovah's Witnesses about the true identity of the "great crowd." Rather, the fact that the Society has taught them wrongly on this important point should be used to open their ears to a presentation of the real gospel of Christ.

This may be introduced by reading Jesus' prayer to the Father at John 17:20–24—"I make request, not concerning these only, but also concerning those putting faith in me through their word. . . . Father, as to what you have given me, I wish that, where I am, they also may be with me, in order to behold my glory . . ." (NWT). Jesus' prayer is that all of his present and future disciples would end up with him, where he is, to behold his glory. Show the Witnesses that the prayer applies to all future disciples who would put faith in Christ through the writings left behind by the early disciples (v. 20). Tell them that, if they will put faith in him, Jesus wants them to end up with him in the heavenly kingdom—regardless of whether they became believers before or after the year 1935.

See also the discussions of heaven *versus* earth at Psalms 37:9, 115:16, and John 10:16; the discussion of communion at Matthew 26:27; and an actual encounter with Jehovah's Witnesses over this issue at Revelation 19:1.

Revelation 19:1

> After these things I heard what was as a loud voice of a great crowd in heaven. (NWT)

Watchtower brainwashing is so powerful that those under its spell can look at black and see white—if the Society says that black is white. That this is no exaggeration was demonstrated in an encounter that I had with a Jehovah's Witness lady who knocked at my door in the summer of 1983. (She did not realize that I was a former member. Otherwise, she would not have spoken a word to me.) The discussion went like this:

David Reed: "I've heard that you people believe that you are part of a 'great crowd' who will receive everlasting life on earth, instead of going to heaven. Is that true? Can you show me the 'great crowd' in the Bible?"

Mrs. Jehovah's Witness: "Yes, that is what the Bible says. See, here it is at Revelation 7:9. [She reads the verse discussed above, at Rev. 7:9.] I hope to be part of that 'great crowd' that will live on earth forever."

David Reed: "But Revelation 7:15 places the 'great crowd' before the throne of God in heaven, doesn't it?"

Mrs. Jehovah's Witness: "Well, the throne of God is in heaven, but the 'great crowd' is on the earth. All creation stands before the throne of God."

David Reed: "I don't think the verse would mention their location before the throne if it meant it in such a general sense. But there is one other place where Revelation talks about the 'great crowd.' Would you please read Revelation 19:1 in your own Bible to see where it locates the 'great crowd'?"

Mrs. Jehovah's Witness: "Certainly! It says, 'After these things I heard what was as a loud voice of a great crowd in heaven.'"

David Reed: "A 'great crowd' *where?*"

Mrs. Jehovah's Witness: "The 'great crowd' is on earth!"

David Reed: "Is that what the verse says? Read it again."

Mrs. Jehovah's Witness: "It says *heaven,* but the 'great crowd' is on *earth.*"

David Reed: "How can you say that the 'great crowd' is on earth, when the Bible plainly says 'a great crowd in *heaven*'?"

Mrs. Jehovah's Witness: "You don't understand. We have men at our headquarters in Brooklyn, New York, who explain the Bible to us. And they can prove that the 'great crowd' is on earth; I just can't explain it that well. Wait just a moment."

At that point she ran out into the street and shouted to another Witness woman, who was a few houses away, to come help her. This woman recognized me as an ex-Witness, and that ended the conversation. But the point had already been illustrated: A JW can look at the word *heaven* in the Bible but see *earth* instead, if the organization says so.

As the two ladies walked away from my doorstep, my mind raced back to memories of George Orwell's novel *Nineteen Eighty-Four.* I recalled the frightening portrayal of a totalitarian state where everyone knows that "Big Brother is watching you!"—and so, "Whatever the Party holds to be truth *is* truth," and "Two plus two equals five, instead of four, if the Party says so." Truly, the Watchtower Society imposes that same sort of "double-think" on Jehovah's Witnesses.

(A number of other parallels between the JW's and the fictional society of *Nineteen Eighty-Four* are highlighted in Gary and Heather Botting's book *The Orwellian World of Jehovah's Witnesses,* 1984, University of Toronto Press).

For further information on the question of heaven *versus* earth, see the discussions of John 10:16 and Revelation 7:9. For other examples of brainwashing, see the discussions of Matthew 24:45; 1 Corinthians 1:10; and "The Author's Testimony."

5

A Capsule History of Jehovah's Witnesses

1879 Charles Taze Russell begins publishing his magazine, *Zion's Watch Tower and Herald of Christ's Presence*

1881 Zion's Watch Tower Tract Society formed

1885 Society reports 300 "colporteurs" distributing literature

1886 Russell publishes his book, *The Divine Plan of the Ages*

1914 Armageddon fails to occur as prophesied

1916 Charles T. Russell dies

1917 "Judge" J. F. Rutherford assumes control of organization

1920 Society proclaims "Millions now living will never die!" and prophesies earthly resurrection to occur in 1925

1920 Organization reports 8,402 volunteers distributing Watchtower literature

1925 Earthly resurrection of Abraham, Isaac, Jacob, *et al.*, fails to occur as prophesied

1927 Watchtower factory is constructed in Brooklyn, New York

1930 "Beth Sarim" built in San Diego to house soon-to-be-resurrected prophets; "Judge" Rutherford lives there

1931 The name "Jehovah's Witnesses" officially adopted

1935 Watchtower Society begins gathering "great crowd"; teaches them earthly hope, no share in communion

1938 Local JW congregations end democratic church government; submit to "theocratic" appointment of all local congregation officials by Brooklyn headquarters

1938 Organization reports 59,047 distributing literature; 69,345 attend annual communion; 36,732 partake

1942 J. F. Rutherford dies; N. H. Knorr becomes President

1943 N. H. Knorr institutes training programs for foreign missionaries and local volunteer workers

1948 Organization reports 260,756 distributing literature; 376,393 attend annual communion; 25,395 partake

1950 *New World Translation* of New Testament published, calling Jesus "a god," inserting "Jehovah" in New Testament

1958 Organization reports 798,326 distributing literature; 1,171,789 attend annual communion; 15,037 partake

1968 *The Watchtower*'s article "Why Are You Looking Forward to 1975?" prophesies likelihood of Armageddon for that year

1975 Organization reports 2,179,256 distributing literature; 4,925,643 attend annual communion; 10,550 partake

1975 Armageddon fails to occur as prophesied

1985 Organization reports 3,024,131 distributing literature; 7,792,109 attend annual communion; 9,051 partake

6

Techniques for Sharing the Gospel with Jehovah's Witnesses

"I was gunning for the next JW to darken my doorstep. As soon as he came, I fired one Scripture verse after another at him. You should have seen him dance! Then I let him have John 1:1 right between the eyes and blew him away!" Do you know someone who had an encounter like that with the Witnesses? If so, he may have won the battle but lost the war.

After a scriptural shoot-out like the above, the wounded and bleeding Witness runs back to his "elders" for protection and comfort. They patch him up by explaining away the damaging verses and warn him not to listen to "argumentative" householders again in the door-to-door preaching work. "Don't worry!" he replies. "I never want to go through something like *that* again."

This volume contains plenty of ammunition for waging spiritual warfare against the Watchtower fortress. But if the Christian warrior corners an individual Jehovah's Witness and lets him have it with both barrels in rapid-fire succession, the result is likely to be disappointing. Since even the JW leaders know that the human mind can absorb only so much information at one time, they instruct Witnesses to plan on at least a six-month "study" with people they are trying to convert. Only the inexperienced Witness will bombard a householder with an Adam-to-Armageddon sermon on the first visit. The JW's are correct in their techniques, and that's one reason for the amazing growth of their organization. So, we do well to learn from them—not their false doctrines, of course, but their effective methods.

However, the best example we can turn to for techniques is our Lord Jesus Christ. As the Master Teacher, he used well-chosen words as well as miracles to draw men to himself. Since he had to teach some startling new concepts to the Jews who became his disciples, we can learn much from his example, in our efforts to share the true gospel with Jehovah's Witnesses.

Jesus knew how much his listeners would be able to absorb at one time, and he didn't try to overfeed them. Even after he had spent many months with the apostles, he told them: "I still have many things to say to you, but you cannot bear them now" (John 16:12, NKJV). The gospel consists of both "milk" and "solid food" (Heb. 5:12–14). If you give solid food to a baby too soon, he will choke on it and spit it out. Realizing that it may take a long time for a Jehovah's Witness to un-learn false Watchtower doctrines and re-learn Bible truth, we should not give him too much to digest at one time.

Jesus could leave much of what he had to say until later, because he knew that the Holy Spirit would continue to teach the disciples—that "when He, the Spirit of truth, has come, He will guide you into all truth . . ." (John 16:13, NKJV). We, too, should trust that the Holy Spirit will teach new believers today, just as in the first century. We need not take it upon ourselves to correct every notion that a Witness has in his head. The Holy Spirit will take over where we leave off.

Moreover, Jesus was a shepherd—not a cowboy! He did not ride herd on the sheep, shooting guns and cracking

114

whips like cowboys do in a cattle drive. No. He gently led the flock. Jesus called, and his sheep heard his voice and followed him. We can do the same by kindly presenting the gospel from the Word of God, confident that the sheep will hear and follow without our having to bully them into it. Jehovah's Witnesses are accustomed to being bullied by their elders; we should stand out in contrast.

Notice, too, the teaching methods that Jesus used. Glancing quickly over any one of the four Gospel accounts, you will observe that many of his sentences had question marks at the end. Question marks are shaped like hooks— " ? "—and they function much the same way in hooking on to answers and pulling them out through the other person's mouth. Jesus was highly skilled at using these fishing hooks. Rather than shower his listeners with information, he used questions to draw answers out of them. A person can close his ears to facts he doesn't want to hear, but if a pointed question causes him to form the answer in his own mind, he cannot escape the conclusion—because it's a conclusion that he reached himself.

On the other hand, if *we* provide the answers, the effect can be quite different. For example, we can tell a Jehovah's Witness: "You have been deceived!" "The Watchtower organization is a false prophet!" "You need to get saved!" But, if the Witness has not yet reached those conclusions in his own mind, he is likely to become offended and reject whatever else we have to say. So, if we want him to reach those conclusions, we must lead his thinking in that direction. Rather than comment, "Look what that verse says! It says Jesus is God!" we could ask the Witness to read the verse aloud and then ask him, "Whom do you think the writer was referring to in this verse? . . . What did he say about him?" and so on. The JW may not say the right answer out loud, but you will see his facial expression change when he gets the point.

Empathy is so very important when reaching out to these misled individuals. Try to think of how you would want others to speak to you, if you were the one who was misled. Then remember that "all things whatsoever ye would that men should do to you, do ye even so to them . . ." (Matt. 7:12, KJV). The apostle Paul demonstrated that sort of empathy in the sermon that he presented to the men of Athens (Acts 17:16–34). Scripture tells us that "his spirit was provoked within him as he saw that the city was full of idols" (v. 16, RSV). But, instead of letting that provocation spill out in a strong rebuke to these idolaters, Paul restrained himself and sought common ground for an appeal to them. He said, "Men of Athens, I perceive that in every way you are very religious. For as I passed along, and observed the objects of your worship, I found also an altar with this inscription, 'To an unknown god.' What therefore you worship as unknown, this I proclaim to you" (vv. 22–23, RSV). We can do the same by acknowledging to a Jehovah's Witness that we appreciate his zeal and his desire to serve God.

A few years ago two young Mormon missionaries contacted my wife, and she made an appointment for them to visit us. In the course of the discussion that evening, I "laid all our cards on the table" and strongly challenged them on the authenticity of the Book of Mormon. They were visibly shaken by the time they left, but we never heard from them again. More recently, two different Mormon boys contacted us, and we set up another appointment. But this time I applied some of the principles outlined in this chapter, feeding them information gently, a little bit at a time. As a result, we had a whole series of visits with them, giving us opportunity to plant much more seed, which we pray will be watered and will grow under God's direction (1 Cor. 3:6–7).

Our more successful approach the second time around reminds me of the story of a young boy whom others in the neighborhood used to tease, calling him retarded. Knowing that the boy was really quite intelligent, an elderly neighbor inquired of the other boys why they teased him so. "Oh, we have fun with him because he's so dumb," one youngster replied. "If you hold a nickel in one hand and a dime in the other, and offer them both to him, he will take the nickel because it looks bigger. He'll do it every time!" Later on, the elderly gentleman called the "retarded" boy over and asked him why he took the nickel. "That's easy," the child replied. "Some weeks I end up with a pocket full of nickels. But, if I took the dime, that would be the end of the game!"

So, whether it's a matter of slowly collecting nickels, or finding common ground, or using probing questions, or saving some points for another time—or even a combination of all of these techniques when appropriate—we should give prayerful thought to our approach, so as to smooth the way for our message to reach the hearts and minds of our listeners.

And, above all, our hope for success should rest in the Lord rather than in ourselves, no matter how much preparation and study we may have done.

> For the weapons of our warfare are not physical, but they are powerful with God's help for the tearing down of fortresses, inasmuch as we tear down reasonings and every proud barrier that is raised up against the knowledge of God and lead every thought into subjection to Christ. (2 Cor. 10:4–5, MLB)

7

The Author's Testimony

My early religious training was in a big, white Unitarian church in rural New England, just south of Boston. I still remember the time when, in my boyish innocence, I expressed to the pastor my belief that God had actually parted the Red Sea to let Moses and the Israelites pass through. He turned to the assistant pastor and said with a laugh, "This boy has a lot to learn." As I grew older I did, in fact, learn what this church taught. Encountering their pamphlet, *What Unitarians Believe,* I read that "Some Unitarians believe in God, and some do not"—and quickly realized the ministers must have been among those who did not believe.

By the time I was fourteen years old, I had reached my own conclusion that religion was "the opium of the people," a convenient thought for an adolescent who preferred not to have God watching him all the time. And when I went on to Harvard University, I found that atheism and agnosticism flourished there, too. So, between the Unitarian church and my Ivy League schooling, I seldom encountered any strong pressure to believe in God.

By the time I was twenty-two, though, I had thought through atheistic evolution to its ultimate end: a pointless existence, followed by death. After all, if humans were nothing more than the last in a series of chemical and

119

biological accidents, then any meaning or purpose we might try to find in life would just be a self-deceptive fiction produced in our own minds. It would have no real connection with the harsh, cold reality of a universe where nothing really mattered. So, I saw myself faced with two choices: God or suicide. Since suicide would be an easy way out for me (I believed there was nothing after death) but would leave those who cared about me to face the pain I would cause, I began to think about God.

Coincidentally (perhaps?), a Jehovah's Witness was assigned to work alongside me at my job. Since God was on my mind, I began asking him questions about his beliefs. His answers amazed me. It was the first time that I had ever heard religious thoughts presented in a tight-knit logical framework. Everything that he said fit together. Since he had an answer for every question, I kept coming up with more questions. Before long, he was conducting a study with me twice a week in the Watchtower Society's new (1968) book *The Truth That Leads to Eternal Life.*

In no time I became a very zealous Witness. After receiving my initial indoctrination and getting baptized, I served as a full-time "pioneer minister." This required that I spend at least one hundred hours each month preaching from house to house and conducting home Bible studies— actually a commitment of much more than a hundred hours, since travel time could not be included in my monthly field-service report. I kept on "pioneering" until 1971, when I married Penni, who had been raised in the organization and who also "pioneered."

My zeal for Jehovah and my proficiency in preaching were rewarded after a few years with appointment as an elder. In that capacity I taught the 150-odd people in my home congregation on a regular basis and made frequent visits to other congregations as a Sunday-morning speaker. Occasionally, I also received assignments to speak to audiences ranging in the thousands at Jehovah's Witness assemblies.

Other responsibilities I carried included presiding over the other local elders, handling correspondence between the local congregation and the Society's Brooklyn headquarters, and serving on judicial committees set up to deal with cases of wrongdoing in the congregation. (I can recall disfellowshiping people for such varied offenses as selling drugs at Kingdom Hall, smoking cigarettes, wife swapping, and having a Christmas decoration in the home.)

Although we were not able to continue "pioneering" after our marriage, Penni and I remained very zealous for the preaching work. Between the two of us, we conducted home Bible studies with dozens of people and brought well over twenty of them into the organization as baptized Jehovah's Witnesses. We also put "the Kingdom" first in our personal lives by keeping our secular employment to a minimum and living in an inexpensive three-room apartment in order to be able to devote more time to the door-to-door preaching activity.

What interrupted this life of full dedication to the Watchtower organization and caused us to enter a path that would lead us out? In one word, it was *Jesus*. Let me explain:

When Penni and I were at a large Witness convention, we saw a handful of opposers picketing outside. One of them carried a sign that said, "READ THE BIBLE, NOT THE WATCHTOWER." We had no sympathy for the picketers, but we did feel convicted by this sign, because we knew that we had been reading Watchtower publications to the exclusion of reading the Bible. (Later on, we actually counted up all the material that the organization expected Witnesses to read. The books, magazines, lessons, and so on, added up to over three thousand pages each year, compared with less than two hundred pages of Bible reading assigned—and most of that was in the Old Testament. The majority of Witnesses were so bogged down by the three thousand pages of the organization's literature that they never got around to doing the Bible reading.)

121

After seeing the picket sign, Penni turned to me and said, "We should be reading the Bible *and* the Watchtower material." I agreed, and we began doing regular personal Bible reading.

That's when we began to think about Jesus. Not that we began to question the Watchtower's teaching that Christ was just Michael the archangel in human flesh—it didn't even occur to us to question that. But we were really impressed with Jesus as a person: what he said and did, how he treated people. We wanted to be his followers. Especially, we were struck with how Jesus responded to the hypocritical religious leaders of the day, the Scribes and Pharisees. I remember reading, over and over again, the accounts relating how the Pharisees objected to Jesus' healing on the Sabbath, his disciples' eating with unwashed hands, and other details of behavior that violated their traditions. How I loved Jesus' response: "You hypocrites, Isaiah aptly prophesied about you, when he said, 'This people honors me with their lips, yet their heart is far removed from me. It is in vain that they keep worshiping me, because they teach commands of men as doctrines' " (Matt. 15:7–9, NWT).

Commands of men as doctrines! That thought stuck in my mind. And I began to realize that, in fulfilling my role as an elder, I was acting more like a Pharisee than a follower of Jesus. For example, the elders were the enforcers of all sorts of petty rules about dress and grooming. We told "sisters" how long they could wear their dresses, and we told "brothers" how to comb their hair, how to trim their sideburns, and what sort of flare or taper they could wear in their pants. We actually told people that they could not please God unless they conformed. It reminded me of the Pharisees who condemned Jesus' disciples for eating with unwashed hands.

My own dress and grooming conformed to the letter. But I ran into problems with newly interested young men whom I brought to Kingdom Hall. Instead of telling them to buy a white shirt and sport coat and to cut their hair short, I told them, "Don't be disturbed if people at Kingdom Hall dress and groom a little on the old-fashioned side. You can continue as you are. God doesn't judge people by their haircut or their clothing." But that didn't work. Someone else would tell them to get a haircut or offer to give them a white shirt—or they would simply feel so out of place that they left, never to return.

This upset me, because I believed their life depended on joining "God's organization." If we Witnesses acted like Pharisees to the point of driving young people away from the only way to salvation, their innocent blood would be on our hands. Talking to the other elders about it didn't help. They felt that the old styles were inherently righteous. But then Jesus' example came to mind:

> And he went on from there, and entered their synagogue. And behold, there was a man with a withered hand. And they asked him, "Is it lawful to heal on the sabbath?" so that they might accuse him. He said to them, "What man of you, if he has one sheep and it falls into a pit on the sabbath, will not lay hold of it and lift it out? Of how much more value is a man than a sheep! So it is lawful to do good on the sabbath." Then he said to the man, "Stretch out your hand" . . . . (Matt. 12:9–13, RSV)

If I were truly to follow Jesus, instead of men, I saw only one course open to me. I personally violated the tradition of the elders by letting my hair grow a half-inch over my ears. My reasoning was: How can they pressure a newcomer to get a haircut, now, with one of the elders wearing the same style?

Well, the other elders reacted the same way the Pharisees did when Jesus told the man to stretch out his hand. Scripture says they "went out and took counsel against him, how to destroy him" (Matt. 12:14, RSV). It took them a while to react, but the elders actually put me on trial, called in witnesses to testify, and spent dozens of hours discussing half an inch of hair.

Grooming was not the real issue, however. For me it was a question of whose disciple I was. Was I a follower of Jesus or an obedient servant to a human hierarchy? The elders who put me on trial knew that that was the real issue, too. They kept asking, "Do you believe that the Watchtower Society is God's organization? Do you believe that the Society speaks as Jehovah's mouthpiece?" At that time I answered *Yes* because I still did believe it was God's organization—but that it had become corrupt, like the Jewish religious system at the time when Jesus was opposed by the Pharisees.

It was what I said at the congregation meetings that got me into real trouble, though. I was still an elder, so— when I was assigned to give a fifteen-minute talk on the Book of Zechariah at the Thursday night Theocratic Ministry School meeting—I took advantage of the opportunity to encourage the audience to read the Bible. In fact, I told them that if their time was limited and they had to choose between reading the Bible and reading *The Watchtower* magazine, they should choose the Bible, because it was inspired by God while *The Watchtower* was not inspired and often taught errors that had to be corrected later.

Not surprisingly, that was the last time they allowed me to give a talk. But I could still speak from my seat during question-and-answer periods at the meetings. We were all expected to answer in our own words, but not in our own thoughts. You were to give the thought found in the paragraph of the lesson being discussed. But, after I said a few things they did not like, they stopped giving me the microphone.

With the new perspective that I was gaining from Bible reading, it upset me to see the organization elevate itself above Scripture, as it did when the December 1, 1981, *Watchtower* said: "Jehovah God has also provided his visible organization. ... Unless we are in touch with this channel of communication that God is using, we will not progress along the road to life, no matter how much Bible reading we do" (p. 27, §4). It really disturbed me to see those men elevate themselves above God's Word. Since I could not speak out at the meetings, I decided to try writing.

That's when I started publishing the newsletter *Comments from the Friends*. I wrote articles questioning what the organization was teaching and signed them with the pen name "Bill Tyndale, Jr."—a reference to sixteenth-century English Bible translator William Tyndale, who was burned at the stake for what he wrote. To avoid getting caught, Penni and I drove across the state line at night to an out-of-state post office and mailed the articles in unmarked envelopes. We sent them to local Witnesses and also to hundreds of Kingdom Halls all across the country, whose addresses we had obtained from telephone books at the town library.

Penni and I knew that we had to leave the Jehovah's Witnesses. But, to us, it was similar to the question of what to do in a burning apartment building. Do you escape through the nearest exit? Or do you bang on doors first, waking the neighbors and helping them escape, too? We felt an obligation to help others get out—especially our families and our "students" whom we had brought into the organization. If we had just walked out, our families left behind would have been forbidden to associate with us.

But, after a few weeks, a friend discovered what I was doing and turned me in. So, one night when Penni and I were returning home from conducting a Bible study, two elders stepped out of a parked car, accosted us in the street, and questioned us about the newsletter. They wanted to put us on trial for publishing it, but we simply stopped going to the Kingdom Hall. By that time most of our former friends there had become quite hostile toward us.

One young man called on the phone and threatened to "come over and take care of" me if he got another one of our newsletters. And another Witness actually left a couple of death threats on our answering machine. The elders went ahead and tried us *in absentia* and disfellowshiped us.

Although it was a great relief to be out from under the oppressive yoke of that organization, we now had to face the immediate challenge of where to go and what to believe. It takes some time to re-think your entire religious outlook on life. Before leaving the Watchtower, we had rejected the claims that the organization was God's "channel of communication," that Christ returned invisibly in the year 1914, and that the "great crowd" of believers since 1935 should not partake of the communion loaf and cup. But we were only beginning to re-examine other doctrines. And we had not yet come into fellowship with Christians outside the JW organization.

All Penni and I knew was that we wanted to follow Jesus and that the Bible contained all the information we needed. So we really devoted ourselves to reading the Bible and to prayer. We also invited our families and remaining friends to meet in our apartment on Sunday mornings. While the Witnesses gathered at Kingdom Hall to hear a lecture and study the *Watchtower* magazine, we met to read the Bible. As many as fifteen attended—mostly family but also some friends.

We were just amazed at what we found in prayerfully reading the New Testament over and over again—things that we had never appreciated before, such as the closeness that the early disciples had with the risen Lord, the activity of the Holy Spirit in the early church, and Jesus' words about being "born again."

All those years as Jehovah's Witnesses, the Watchtower organization had taken us on a guided tour through the Bible. We gained a lot of knowledge about the Old Testament, and we could quote a lot of Scripture, but we never heard the gospel of salvation in Christ. We never learned to depend on Jesus for our salvation and to look to him personally as our Lord. Everything centered around the Watchtower's works program, and people were expected to come to Jehovah God through the organization.

When I realized from reading Romans 8 and John 3 that I needed to be "born of the Spirit," I was afraid at first. Jehovah's Witnesses believe that born-again people, who claim to have the Holy Spirit, are actually possessed by demons. And so I feared that if I prayed out loud to turn my life over to Jesus Christ, some demon might be listening; and the demon might jump in and possess me, pretending to be the Holy Spirit. (Many Jehovah's Witnesses live in constant fear of the demons. Some of our friends would even throw out furniture and clothing, fearing that the demons could enter their homes through those articles.) But then I read Jesus' words at Luke 11:9–13. In a context where he was teaching about prayer and casting out unclean spirits, Jesus said:

> And I say to you, ask, and it will be given to you; seek, and you will find; knock, and it will be opened to you. For everyone who asks receives, and he who seeks finds, and to him who knocks it will be opened. If a son asks for bread from any father among you, will he give him a stone? Or if he asks for a fish, will he give him a serpent instead of a fish? Or if he asks for an egg, will he offer him a scorpion? If you then, being evil, know how to give good gifts to your children, how much more will your heavenly Father give the Holy Spirit to those who ask Him! (NKJV).

I knew, after reading those words, that I could safely ask for Christ's Spirit (Rom. 8:9), without fearing that I would receive a demon. So, in the early morning privacy of our kitchen, I proceeded to confess my need for salvation and to commit my life to Christ.

127

About a half hour later, I was on my way to work, and I was about to pray again. It had been my custom for many years to start out my prayers by saying, "Jehovah God . . . ." But this time, when I opened my mouth to pray, I started out by saying, "Father. . . ." It was not because I had reasoned on the subject and reached the conclusion that I should address God differently; the word *Father* just came out, without my even thinking about it. Immediately, I understood why: "God has sent forth the Spirit of His Son into your hearts, crying out, 'Abba, Father!' " (Gal. 4:6, NKJV). I wept with joy at God's confirmation of this new and more intimate relationship with him.

Penni and I soon developed the desire to worship and praise the Lord in a congregation of believers and to benefit from the wisdom of mature Christians. Since the small group of ex-Witnesses was still meeting in our apartment on Sunday mornings for Bible reading, and most of them were not yet ready to venture into a church, we began visiting churches that had evening services. One church we attended was so legalistic that we almost felt as though we were back in the Kingdom Hall. Another was so liberal that the sermon always seemed to be on philosophy or politics—instead of on Jesus. Finally, though, the Lord led us to a congregation where we felt comfortable, and where the focus was on Jesus Christ and his gospel, rather than on side issues.

Penni now teaches fifth grade in a Christian school that has students from about seventeen different churches. She really enjoys it, because she can tie in the Scriptures with all sorts of subjects. And, besides my secular job, I continue publishing *Comments from the Friends* as a quarterly newsletter aimed at reaching Jehovah's Witnesses with the gospel and helping Christians who are talking to JW's. It also contains articles of special interest to ex-Witnesses. Subscribers are found in a dozen foreign countries, as well as all across the United States and Canada. Besides writing on the subject, I speak occasionally to church groups interested in learning how to answer Jehovah's Witnesses so as to lead them to Christ.

We also provide a weekly phone-in recorded message for Jehovah's Witnesses. Twenty-four hours a day, JW's can call 617-584-4467 and hear a brief message directing them to the Bible and helping them to disprove Watchtower teachings. Some Witnesses even call during the middle of the night, so that their family members will not observe and report them to the elders. So far, we have received over six thousand calls. At the end of each message the caller is invited to leave his or her name and address so as to receive free literature in the mail—and many do.

The thrust of our outreach ministry is to help Jehovah's Witnesses break free from deception and put faith in the original gospel of Christ as it is presented in the Bible. The most important lesson Penni and I learned since leaving the Jehovah's Witnesses is that Jesus is not just a historical figure whom we read about. He is alive and is actively involved with Christians today, just as he was back in the first century. He personally saves us, teaches us, and leads us. This personal relationship with God through his Son, Jesus Christ, is so wonderful! The individual who knows Jesus and follows him will not even think about following anyone else:

> "A stranger they will not follow, but they will flee from him, for they do not know the voice of strangers. . . . My sheep hear my voice, and I know them, and they follow me; and I give them eternal life, and they shall never perish, and no one shall snatch them out of my hand." (John 10:5, 27–28, RSV)

The author is interested in your questions and observations on the material found in this book. You may write him c/o *Comments from the Friends,* P.O. Box 840, Stoughton, MA 02072.

Bibliography

Watchtower Society Literature

Zion's Watch Tower and Herald of Christ's Presence (reprints), 1879

The Divine Plan of the Ages, C. T. Russell, 1886

Millions Now Living Will Never Die, J. F. Rutherford, 1920

Jehovah's Witnesses in the Divine Purpose, 1959

The Truth That Leads to Eternal Life, 1968

You Can Live Forever in Paradise on Earth, 1982

Enjoy Life on Earth Forever!, 1982

Reasoning from the Scriptures, 1985

Yearbook of Jehovah's Witnesses, 1949, 1959, 1976

The Watchtower (various issues)

Works Critical of the Watchtower Movement

Apocalypse Delayed: The Story of Jehovah's Witnesses, M. James Penton (Univ. of Toronto Press, 1985)

Crisis of Conscience, Raymond Franz (Commentary Press, 1983)

Dialogue with Jehovah's Witnesses, Duane Magnani and Arthur Barrett (Witness, Inc., 1983)

I Was Raised a Jehovah's Witness, Joe Hewitt (Accent Books, 1979)

Jehovah's Witnesses: Watch Out for the Watchtower! Gordon E. Duggar (Baker Book House, 1985)

Out of Darkness Into Light: A Jehovah's Witness Finds the Truth in Jesus Christ, Peter Barnes (Equippers, 1984)

Questions for Jehovah's Witnesses Who Love the Truth, William I. Cetnar (self-published, 1983)

Scripture Twisting: 20 Ways the Cults Misread the Bible, James W. Sire (InterVarsity Press, 1980)

The Jehovah's Witnesses' New Testament, Robert H. Countess (Presbyterian and Reformed Pub. Co., 1982)

The Kingdom of the Cults, Walter Martin (Bethany House, 1986)

The Orwellian World of Jehovah's Witnesses, Heather and Gary Botting (Univ. of Toronto Press, 1984)

Thus Saith . . . the Governing Body of Jehovah's Witnesses, Randall Watters (Bethel Ministries, 1984)

Unholy Devotion: Why Cults Lure Christians, Harold Busséll (Zondervan, 1983)

Who's That Knocking At My Door? Alex Nova (self-published, 1978)

Cassette Tapes

Jehovah's Witnesses and the Deity of Christ, Peter Barnes (Equippers, 1983)

Subject Index

Scripture Index

Scripture Index

Acts

1:5—85
1:8—45
2:4—80, 85–87
2:33—85
4:10–12—29
5:3–4—22, 52, 80, 86–87, 90, 95
5:29—15
7:57—88
7:59–60—87
10:45—85
12:28–29—23, 30
13:2—22, 86
14:13—95
15:1, 2—54
15:28–29—88
17:16—116
17:16–34—116
17:22–23—116
19:35—95

Romans

3:26—106
6:3—51
8—75, 76, 89, 127
8:1–7—75
8:8–9—75, 89–90
8:9—127
8:14–16—75
8:14–39—81
8:15—29
8:26–27—22, 52, 87, 90
10:2–3—8
14:1—94
14:2–5—93
14:5–6—94
14:7, 8—91
14:7–9—69, 90–92
14:8–9—19
14:9—91

1 Corinthians

1:10—92–94, 110
3:6—76

3:6–7—116
6:19—22, 24, 52, 62, 80, 86, 87, 90, 95
8:1–13—88
8:4—36
8:5—42, 71
8:6—24, 95–96
10:16–17—106
10:25—89
10:27—88
11:3—96–97
12:13—106
12:27—106
13:12—82

2 Corinthians

3:17—82, 86
4:4—42, 71
5:1—46
5:8–10—46
10:4–5—117

Galatians

1:8–9—56
3:27—51
4:5–6—74
4:5–9—81
4:6—29, 128

Ephesians

1:23—86
6:17—9
13:12—24

Philippians

1:23–24—41
2:6–7—80
2:9–11—29
2:17—85

Colossians

1:15—49, 97–98
1:18—97

2:9—24, 62, 76, 97–98, 103
3:14—94

1 Thessalonians

4:16—47

2 Timothy

3:7—81
3:16–17—98–100
3:17—100
4:6—85
4:18—106

Hebrews

1—47–48
1:2–8—48
1:3—43, 48
1:6—19, 48, 69, 74, 76, 77, 100, 101
1:10—48, 84
2:9—80
3:1—37
5:12–14—114
11:13—79
11:16—79
12:22—79
12:24—60, 106

2 Peter

3:16—17

1 John

5:1—74

Jude

4—82
9—47

Revelation

1:7–8—24, 43, 49, 62, 80, 82, 85, 96, 97, 98, 101–03
1:17–18—103